W9-BWM-470

Jesuit Life & Mission Today

The Decrees
& Accompanying Documents of the
36th General Congregation
of the Society of Jesus

Institute of Jesuit Sources
Boston College

This North-American publication of the documents of the Thirty-Sixth General Congregation of the Society of Jesus is an edited English-language version of the official texts produced in Rome by the General Curia of the Society of Jesus.

Library of Congress Control Number: 2017002959

ISBN: 978-0-9972823-5-1

Institute of Jesuit Sources
at the Institute for Advanced Jesuit Studies
Boston College
140 Commonwealth Avenue | Chestnut Hill, MA 02467 | USA

email: iajs@bc.edu
http://jesuitsources.bc.edu

Fees are subject to change

**INSTITUTE FOR
ADVANCED JESUIT STUDIES**
BOSTON COLLEGE

Institute of Jesuit Sources
Boston College

Contents

Letter of Promulgation of the Decrees 1

Historical Introduction 3

Decrees

Decree 1: Companions in a Mission of Reconciliation and Justice 17

Decree 2: Renewed Governance for a Renewed Mission 27

Other Documents 37

Witnesses of Friendship and Reconciliation: A Message and a
Prayer for Jesuits Living in Zones of War and Conflict 37

Matters Entrusted to Father General 41

Modification of *Constitutions* 701 and 704 42

Revision of *Complementary Norm* 362 42

Revision of *Complementary Norm* 396 43

Complementary Documentation 45

Address of His Holiness Pope Francis to the
36th General Congregation of the Society of Jesus 45

Dialogue of Pope Francis with the Jesuits Gathered in the
36th General Congregation 53

Words of Gratitude to Fr. Adolfo Nicolás, S.J. 65

Homily of Fr. Bruno Cadoré, O.P. 70

Homily of Fr. James E. Grummer, S.J. 73

Homily of Fr. Arturo Sosa, S.J.: Mass of Thanksgiving 76

Homily of Fr. Arturo Sosa, S.J.: Closure of the General
Congregation 36th 78

GC 36: List of Participants 80

Index 85

CURIA GENERALIZIA DELLA COMPAGNIA DI GESÙ

36th General Congregation:
Promulgation of the Decrees (2017/01)

To the Whole Society

Dear Brothers in Christ,

The Peace of Christ!

The promulgation of the Decrees of the 36th General Congregation is an important step in the process of discernment of our life and mission as companions of Jesus, a process that began when the 36th General Congregation was convoked. Each one of us, as well as the communities of the Society and its apostolic works, placed ourselves in readiness to discern the call made to us today by the Lord amidst the cry of the peoples of the earth for a more humane life. The Province Congregations were a moment in which the call was heard, with openness of mind and spirit. Their contributions, in conjunction with the numerous postulates received, paved the way for continued reflection to prepare the ground for the communal discernment of the Society of Jesus, gathered in General Congregation.

We have lived an experience of discernment nourished by the preparatory work, the fraternal dialogue with the Holy Father Pope Francis, the personal prayer and reflection of each of the delegates, the community prayer, the Eucharist and the work of the whole assembly. The conviction that our life and mission must be closely integrated in order to truly incarnate the promotion of justice, by striving for reconciliation in all its dimensions as an imperative of our faith, animated all the deliberations during the six weeks of GC 36. The decrees reflect this spirit and the implications that are drawn for our structures of government.

Through this letter, in compliance with the decision taken by the 36th General Congregation in its final session on November 12, 2016, and according to No. 142 of the *Formula*, I am pleased to promulgate its decrees. They take effect today.

Thus begins the most challenging phase of the process of discernment by the body of the Society of Jesus and those with whom we share the mission. The decrees of GC 36 are an invitation to enter into this phase of making choices in relation to our identity as Jesuits and our way of proceeding in mission. They are an invitation to choose this path, putting ourselves unconditionally at the disposition of the One Who calls us. The success of the Congregation lies in the fruit of our personal conversion, in the necessary changes in the life style of our communities, and in the willingness to be sent to the peripheries or frontiers of the contemporary world to share the joy of the gospel.

Only by confirming that we have placed all our hope in the Lord will we be able to seek and find His will in order to do it, as witnesses of the love of God to all human beings. Mary, our Mother, and her husband, Joseph, showed to those who are simple at heart the marvelous manifestation of God in Jesus, the One born through work of the Holy Spirit. We ask them to show us their Son and open our hearts to this wonderful revelation in order that we may place ourselves entirely at His service.

Arturo Sosa, S.I.
Superior General
Rome, January 6, 2017
Feast of the Epiphany of the Lord

HISTORICAL INTRODUCTION

1. Anticipatory Phase of General Congregation 36

In a letter of 20 May 2014 (2014/08), Father General Adolfo Nicolás informed the whole Society that later in the year he intended to summon a General Congregation. He noted that, after the Assistants *ad providentiam* indicated their support for conducting a formal consultation about convoking a General Congregation, he had informed Pope Francis of his plans. Father Nicolás explained that he had consulted the Provincials and Assistants *ad providentiam* according to the procedure described in *Complementary Norm* 362. Since they had indicated their approval for summoning a General Congregation, he announced the cancellation of the meeting of Provincials that he had previously planned for Yogyakarta in January 2015.

On the feast of the Immaculate Conception, 8 December 2014, Father Nicolás formally convoked the 36th General Congregation. In his letter to the whole Society, he indicated that all Province Congregations should complete their work before 31 July 2015 so that the first plenary session of the General Congregation could begin in Rome on 3 October 2016, the feast of St. Francis Borgia. In addition to encouraging the Province Congregations to deal with any postulates that might emerge, Father Nicolás invited the members to reflect on the three most important calls the Eternal King makes to the whole Society today. He also urged all Jesuits and communities to pray for all the preparations that would culminate in the General Congregation.

Even before the official convocation of the Congregation, Father General established seven working groups within the Curia Generalizia to facilitate preparations for the Congregation. A Postulate Committee [Robert Althann (ZIM), Joaquín Barrero (ESP), Rigobert Kyungu Musenge (ACE), and chair Antoine Kerhuel (GAL)] organized the materials sent by the Province Congregations before the *Coetus Praevius* met. Antoine Kerhuel (GAL) led Lisbert D'Souza (BOM) and Daniel Huang (PHI) in organizing and preparing the work of the official *Coetus Praevius* in anticipation of its arrival. Patrick Mulemi (ZAM) worked with James Grummer (WIS) and Gabriel Ignacio Rodríguez (COL) in addressing issues of Communications. The leader of the Logistics Committee, Arturo Sosa (VEN), called together various members of the Curia community [Lauro Eidt (BRA), Robert Danieluk (PMA), Jesús Rodríguez (UCS), and Gian Giacomo Rotelli (ITA)] to organize the practical details of feeding, housing, and shaping the community of the Electors and Members who attended the Congregation. Ignacio Echarte (ESP) took charge of the Secretariat Committee [Miguel Cruzado (PER) and Tomasz Kot (PMA)] for planning and overseeing the technological and secretarial infrastructure for the Congregation. Severin Leitner (ASR) coordinated the other members of the Liturgy Committee [José Magadia (PHI) and Fratern Masawe (AOR)] in ordering albs, stoles, and vestments for the Congregation participants; organizing the plenary and daily Eucharistic liturgies; and in identifying Clemens Blattert (GER) to lead the daily morning prayers. After the tragic death of Father Leitner, James Grummer (WIS) acted as chair of the group. Chair Thomas McClain (CDT), Daniel Huang, and Douglas Marcouiller (UCS) established procedures and budgets to organize the financial aspects of the Congregation. Father Grummer helped the committees coordinate their tasks to avoid overlapping responsibilities.

In response to GC 35's call for "the presence of an adequate number of Brothers as electors," the Major Superiors and elected members of each Conference elected a Brother from among those nominated by the Province Congregations. The Electors were Ian Cribb (ASL) for CAP-Asia Pacific, Stephen Power (BRI) for EUR-Europe, Thomas Vaz (BOM for JCS-South Asia, Guy J. Consolmagno (MAR) for JCU-Canada and USA, James Edema (AOR) for JES-Africa and Madagascar, and Eudson Ramos (BRA) for PAL-Latin America.

2. The Preparatory Phase of General Congregation 36

In accord with *Formula* 13 and after consultation with the Conference Presidents and the General Council, Father General named the members of the *Coetus Praevius* and summoned them to convene on 31 August 2015 with the task of completing the immediate preparations for the General Congregation. The members of the *Coetus Praevius* were Father Nicolás (*ex officio*), Moderator Douglas Marcouiller (UCS, General Counselor), Paul Béré (AOC, Professor, Institut de Théologie de la Compagnie de Jésus, Abidjan), Jorge Cela (ANT, President of CPAL), John Dardis (HIB, President of CEP), Stefan Dartmann (GER, Rector, Collegio Germanico e Ungarico, Rome), David Fernández (MEX, Rector, Universidad Iberoamericana, Mexico), Thomas Greene (UCS, Rector, Bellarmine House of Studies, St. Louis), Timothy Kesicki (CDT, President of JCU), Michael Lewis (SAF, President of JESAM), Antonio Moreno (PHI, Provincial), George Pattery (CCU, President of JCSA), Francis Xavier Periyanayagam (MDU, Director, Loyola College of Engineering, Chennai), and Mark Raper (ASL, President of JCAP).

The *Coetus Praevius* met 31 August–12 September 2015 to organize, classify, evaluate, and select the themes and postulates that the General Congregation or Father General should address (*FCG* 13, §13). After carefully studying the 146 postulates, 242 Calls, and 20 themes the *Coetus Praevius* received for review and action, the *Coetus* identified the emphasis on integration that emerged from the Province Congregations throughout the world. In every region, Jesuits called for greater integration of the Society's response to the apostolic challenges of today—care for our human, social, and natural environment; solidarity with migrants and other vulnerable peoples; and the construction of a new culture of dialogue and reconciliation. At the same time, the Province Congregations asked the Society to integrate more deeply its spiritual experience, its community life as friends in the Lord, and its apostolic service. The emphasis on integration led the *Coetus* to form two commissions: one focusing on a call to renewal of Jesuit life and mission; the other focusing on renewed governance for a renewed mission.

When Father Nicolás reported to the whole Society about the work of the *Coetus Praevius* (3 October 2015), he presented a summary of the responses that the Provinces and Regions had made to the question, "Meditating on the call of the Eternal King, what do we discern to be the three most important calls that the Lord makes to the whole Society today?" He asked, in particular, that all the communities and ministries of the Society reflect prayerfully on this summary as a way to participate spiritually in the Congregation's process of discernment. Father Nicolás also announced that, in deference to the Holy Father's opinion, the *Coetus* had decided to entrust the small number of postulates calling for reconsideration of grades to the Superior General for a study of options for celebrating final vows.

3. The Initial Phase of General Congregation 36

The *Formula for a General Congregation* initiated by GC 35 indicates that the work of the General Congregation begins when the President of each Conference convenes the Conference Members (*FCG* 14, §1). Meeting independently at different times in October and November 2015 all the Conferences began the initial phase of GC 36. Eventually, the Members from South Asia and those from Africa-Madagascar met a second time as well. As required by the *Formula*, at each Conference meeting the Members discussed the materials provided by the *Coetus Praevius*, considered the state of the Society and other pertinent matters, and shared information about who could be elected General. They also chose one Member for each of the following committees: (1) the Coordinating Committee of the General Congregation; (2) the Deputation *De statu Societatis*; (3) a Commission concerned with "the Renewal of Jesuit Life and Mission"; and (4) a Commission to study "Renewed Governance for a Renewed Mission" (*FCG* 14, §§2–6).

Father General was an *ex officio* member of the Coordinating Committee, and he presided at its meetings. The six men elected at the Conference meetings were the other members of the committee: Paul Béré (AOC), Jorge Cela

(ANT), Stefan Dartmann (GER), Timothy Kesicki (CDT), Antonio Moreno (PHI), and George Pattery (CCU). Immediately after the election of the members of the Coordinating Committee, Father Nicolás called them to their first meeting in Rome, which took place during the first two weeks of December 2015. After the working groups established by Father General provided important background information, the Coordinating Committee began to exercise its responsibility for making decisions about the details of the Congregation.

The Coordinating Committee appointed moderators for the Deputation on the State of the Society [Agbonkhianmeghe Orobator (AOR)], the Commission on the Renewal of Jesuit Life and Mission [Francis Gonsalves (GUJ)], and the Commission on Renewed Governance in the Service of Renewed Mission [Miguel Cruzado (PER)]. In anticipation of the January meetings of the commissions, it established guidelines to help the various groups accomplish their tasks. The Coordinating Committee stressed the importance of working from the perspective of the universal Society rather than a Region or Province, studying and discussing the postulates and themes thoroughly, and the importance of seeking the integration proposed by the *Coetus Praevius*. Furthermore, the Coordinating Committee encouraged each commission to consult experts if they needed further information about a topic. Each commission was free to prepare the text of a possible decree if one might be necessary.

The Coordinating Committee established a Postulate Committee moderated by Douglas Marcouiller (UCS) that included Rigobert Kyungu Musenge (ACE), Bienvenido F. Nebres (PHI), Alfonso Carlos Palacio Larrauri (BRA), Francis Parmar (GUJ), and Nicolas Standaert (CHN). This group performed an invaluable service by studying the 29 personal postulates submitted by individual Jesuits or groups of Jesuits after the first session of the *Coetus Praevius* and the 9 postulates submitted by members of the Congregation before it concluded its business.

The Coordinating Committee also established a Juridical Commission as the *Formula* directed (*FCG* 15, §2, 7°): Robert Geisinger (CDT), Thomas Greene (UCS), Francis Kurien (HAZ), Michael Lewis (SAF), Benoît Malvaux (BML, moderator), and Luis Javier Sarralde Delgado (COL). This group explained changes introduced into the *Formula* since the last Congregation, proposed points for decision by the Congregation, and provided juridical advice on a number of different occasions.

Taking advantage of previously planned meetings, the Coordinating Committee eventually met in late February, mid-August, and late September to continue its planning and coordination of the General Congregation.

The Deputation on the State of the Society included the four Assistants *ad providentiam* [Lisbert D'Souza (BOM), James E. Grummer (WIS), Federico

Lombardi (ITA), and Gabriel Ignacio Rodríguez (COL)] and one man elected by each Conference: John Dardis (HIB), Agbonkhianmeghe Orobator (AOR), Bernardinus Herry Priyono (IDO), Sebasti L. Raj (MDU), Mark Ravizza, (CFN), and Arturo Sosa (VEN).

Those elected to serve as the Commission on the Renewal of Jesuit Life and Mission were Stephen Curtin (ASL), José Ignacio García Jiménez (ESP), Francis Gonsalves (GUJ), Ludovic Lado (AOC), John McCarthy (CDA), and Luís Rafael Velasco (ARU).

Soon after the Conferences met, the commissions received an invitation to attend their initial meeting in Rome. Three groups were able to meet at the Curia in Rome at the same time, 13–16 January 2016: the Deputation on the State of the Society, the Juridical Commission, and the Commission on Life and Mission. The Commission on Mission and Governance met 27–30 January. Each commission had the opportunity to meet with Father General to learn more about their responsibilities and the perspective of the Coordinating Committee. The three groups that had the opportunity to meet at the same time were able to pray and meet together, intensifying the sense that the Congregation was underway and making progress, even before the first plenary session.

During their initial meetings, the deputation and commissions planned their work schedules for the months from January through September so they could study, consult, discern, and write in anticipation of the beginning of the plenary phase of the Congregation. All the groups eventually prepared draft documents for review and comment by the Electors and Members. The electronic system developed at the Curia greatly facilitated this work.

Father Nicolás encouraged a number of practical initiatives to assist the Congregation. To make the Congregation as paperless as possible, Father Ignacio Echarte (ESP) and Mr. Kenneth Yong (director of the Curia's information technology) took advantage of the latest technological innovations as they designed a remarkably successful system. To make the aula as safe as possible, Mr. Fabrizio Salis of the Curia staff assisted Fathers Echarte and Sosa in overseeing a massive renovation project that included installing a new heating and air-conditioning system, devising the best use of wireless technology, and reorienting the seating in the aula. In spite of unforeseen challenges and unanticipated delays, all was ready for a series of training sessions before the first plenary assembly. These enabled the Members to familiarize themselves with the systems for simultaneous translation, accessing electronic documents, voting, and electronic communications. After the Congregation was underway, Edward Fassett (CFN) earned high marks for demonstrating heroic patience as he helped technological tyros overcome various difficulties.

On the evening of 2 October, hundreds of Jesuits and friends of the Society joined the Members of the Congregation for a concelebrated Eucharist at the Church of the Gesù that Washington Paranhos (BRA) planned and coordinated as Master of Ceremonies. A visiting choir directed by Vlastimil Dufka (SVK) prayerfully supported the full and active participation of the entire congregation. Father Bruno Cadoré, Master of the Order of Preachers, presided and preached with eloquence and grace. He spoke eloquently and inspired the participants by inviting them "to move between the duty of constantly calling the Society to dare the audacity of the 'improbable' and the evangelical willingness to do it with the humility of those who know that, in this service where the human engages all his energy, 'everything depends on God.'"

4. First Plenary Sessions of General Congregation 36

The first plenary session of General Congregation 36 began Monday, 3 October with the hymn *Veni Creator Spiritus* and opening prayer with every Elector present. Father Nicolás immediately informed the Electors that he had appointed James E. Grummer (WIS) as Vicar to oversee the proceedings until the election of a new General. Father Grummer then introduced the translators, amanuenses, and technical support staff; on behalf of the Congregation, he thanked them in anticipation for their important contributions to the work of the coming weeks. The Congregation unanimously approved the presence of the support staff and then declared itself complete and legitimate.

Father Grummer presented the daily schedule that the Congregation usually followed throughout the rest of the Congregation. Each day began at 9 AM with a morning prayer that Clemens Blattert (GER) carefully prepared. Clemens Blattert, Gabriel Côté (GLC Elector), José Yuraszeck (CHL student at the Gregorian), and sometimes Jesuit scholastics from San Saba in Rome provided musical accompaniment. Different members of the Congregation led the multilingual prayers that always included a benediction in the local language of the presider. Two morning sessions and two afternoon sessions, each lasting about 75 minutes, preceded the evening liturgies in four different locations to accommodate the Spanish, Italian, French, and English language preferences.

The Vicar noted that the joyful newness of such things as the *Formula*, the aula, the technology, and relationships with brothers from throughout the world should be accompanied by awareness of potential tensions about perspectives and values that the enemy of our human nature might try to exploit as a way to undermine our consolation and peace. He suggested that the Ignatian emphasis in the Spiritual Exercises on generosity [5], reverence [3], and withdrawal from distractions [20] could help the members during the prolonged period of communal discernment.

By a secret electronic ballot the Electors approved the proposal that Agnelo Mascarenhas (GOA) serve as interim secretary of the Congregation until the election of the Secretary of the Congregation. The Electors also agreed that Paul Béré (AOC) and Jorge Cela (ANT) should serve as Examiners in the vote about the General's resignation through an application of *FCG* 46, §2. The Congregation then supplied all deficiencies that might have occurred in the Provincial Congregations or anywhere else.

In the light of *FCG* 31, §3, the Congregation unanimously confirmed that the norms for confidentiality that Father General had determined for the communications team should apply to all. Therefore, the names of individual speakers; the numerical results of votes; and anything not yet resolved or that might change before the end of the General Congregation must remain confidential. Timothy Kesicki (CDT) and John Dardis (HIB) received the mandate to work with the communications team organized by Father Patrick Mulemi (ZAM) about publishing appropriate information.

After the Congregation completed all this business, Father Nicolás presented his resignation in a simple and humble review of the state of his health, emphasizing his desire that the Society have the leadership it needs to serve the Church. Gabriel Ignacio Rodríguez (COL) reported the perspective of the Assistants *ad providentiam* regarding Father Nicolás's health after he left the aula, and the Vicar invited the electors to ask any questions. Since no one raised any further points about the reasons for and against the proposed resignation, the Congregation took a few moments for prayer before proceeding to the secret paper ballot, which accepted the resignation. Father Nicolás received a thunderous and long lasting standing ovation in gratitude for his faithful service of the Society when he returned to the aula. Father Federico Lombardi (ITA) then thanked Father Nicolás on behalf of the Congregation and the Society, presenting him with an icon that Marko Rupnik (SVN) had prepared. Father Nicolás thanked the Congregation and the entire Society for the affection and support he had received during his time in office; then this historic session that had so deeply moved the participants ended.

In the first session of the afternoon, the Vicar informed the Congregation that the Holy Father had already sent his blessing on the Congregation and the election of a new General and that Pope Francis planned to meet with all the Members on 24 October. The Congregation then approved the Vicar's proposal that Lisbert D'Souza (BOM), Regional Assistant for South Asia and Assistant *ad providentiam,* give the exhortation on the day of the election. The Vicar then took a few minutes to explain that during the next few days, on at least 10 different occasions, discussions would prepare the Electors for the discernment at the heart of the Congregation. The discussions in 20 small groups provided time to become more familiar with the materials already prepared for the Congregation (especially the *De statu Societatis*), prepare for the election of the Secretary of the Congregation and his Assistants, and get to know one another more deeply. Thus, the discussion questions would focus on introducing the Members to one another, recognizing the spiritual movements that arose when considering the materials, and providing Members the opportunity to identify important points for further consideration.

Later during the session, on behalf of the Deputation on the State of the Society, Agbonkhianmeghe Orobator (AOR) presented a description of the preparation of the report, its main themes, and suggestions about how to use it in discussions. Finally, after a short break, the Congregation Members divided into 20 small groups to review the *Relatio praevia* and the *Calls*.

Over the next three days, although several important presentations took place in the *aula*, the Congregation primarily conducted its business in small groups. The small groups discussed the situation of the world today, the situation of the Church today, vocation promotion and formation, the Society's universal mission in a global society, the situation of Jesuit community life, servant leadership, collaboration, and the challenges the Society will face in the next ten years. At one afternoon session, the moderator of the Commission on the Renewal of Jesuit Life and Mission, Francis Gonsalves (GUJ), explained how the commission had organized and conducted its work; then he introduced the latest version of a possible decree. The next afternoon, the moderator of the Commission on Renewed Governance for Renewed Mission, Miguel Cruzado (PER), presented a similar survey and introduction.

After the morning prayer on the fourth day of the Congregation, 6 October, the Vicar noted that a few Electors had asked to postpone the date of the election from the initially proposed date of 11 October. He mentioned the importance of examining the movements experienced when considering the reasons for and against a delay. After a brief time of prayer and after working together in raising the reasons for and against the proposal, the Electors prayed again briefly before deciding by an overwhelming majority to begin the *murmuratio* on Monday, 10 October. The Electors then met in small groups to continue the discussion of the *De statu* document.

In a plenary session at the beginning of the afternoon, the Electors had the opportunity to ask questions about the *De statu* report. Father Orobator (AOR), the moderator of the deputation, organized the responses. During the final meeting of the day, four redactors [Francis Xavier Periyanayagam (MDU), José Ignacio García (ESP), Paulin Manwelo (ACE), and Thomas D. Stegman (WIS)] summarized the conversations of the small group discussions about the challenges the Society will face in the next ten years. The Electors took the opportunity to make comments and present reflections until adjournment to celebrate the Eucharist in various languages.

On the fifth day of the Congregation, 7 October, the members made a pilgrimage through the Holy Door for the extraordinary Jubilee Year of Mercy and celebrated the Eucharist together at the Altar of the Chair in the Basilica of St. Peter. Bienvenido Nebres (PHI), the senior religious among the members, presided and preached at a quiet, early morning ceremony while a torrential downpour raged outside. After the usual morning prayer in the aula, the members of the Congregation met in Assistancy groups to prepare two *ternae*, one for the election of the Secretary of the Congregation and one for the election of the assistant secretaries.

In the first afternoon session, the Society's Procurator General, Benoît Malvaux (BML), explained the major changes in the *Formula* that GC 35 had initiated in decree 5, nn. 2–4. After receiving a few clarifications, the members unanimously approved the revised *Formula for a General Congregation*. The Vicar then explained why the Assistants *ad providentiam* and the Coordinating Committee had determined that the proposed changes in *Complementary Norm* 362 did not meet the requirements necessary for discussing the matter before the election of the General. No one made a representation regarding the decision. After a brief discussion, the Electors approved the composition of the Coordinating Committee.

In the final meeting of the day, the Electors assembled for the secret electronic balloting to elect the Secretary of the Congregation and his assistants. Luis Orlando Torres (UCS) was elected Secretary of the Congregation; Agnelo Mascarenhas (GOA) was elected first assistant; and Francisco Javier Álvarez de los Mozos (ESP) was elected second assistant. After a brief prayer of thanksgiving that the Assistancies had nominated so many excellent candidates without consideration of their origins, the Congregation adjourned to celebrate the Eucharist in the various languages.

After the opening prayer of the sixth day of the Congregation Father Grummer announced that the Coordinating Committee had decided upon a method for approving the minutes of the Congregation (*FCG* 23). Jean-Marc Biron (GLC), Nicolas Standaert (CHN), and Scott Santarosa (CFN) would review each day's minutes and approve them on behalf of all the members. The Vicar then asked François-Xavier Dumortier (GAL), Francisco Javier Álvarez de los Mozos (ESP), and Devadoss Mudiappasamy (MDU) to describe their experience of the process for gathering information before the election of the General. Other Electors who had also attended previous Congregations added a few brief points that helped all those present better understand how to proceed.

After a brief pause, Father Grummer read the names of the judges on ambitioning, the Vicar (ACU) and the Electors oldest in religion from each Assistancy: Paramasivam Stanislaus Amalraj (JCS), Jorge Carvajal Cela (ALS), John K. Guiney (EOC), Michael Lewis (AFR), Federico Lombardi (EMR), Anto Lozuk

(ECO), Bienvenido F. Nebres (ASP), and Alfonso Carlos Palacio Larrauri (ALM). He then presented some points for reflection and prayer before the beginning of the election phase of the Congregation. He proposed some points for an Examen of the first week of the Congregation so that the Electors could recognize more deeply the graces received. After celebrating the Eucharist in language groups, the Electors enjoyed a day and a half for relaxation and recreation.

5. The Election Phase of the Congregation

The election phase of the Congregation began with an exhortation by the Vicar on Monday, 10 October. Father Grummer reminded the Electors of the special quality of the four days as a time of reverential recollection and deep respect for each individual and for the way God works so that all might seek God's will with growing confidence. To promote and facilitate the atmosphere of prayer, the Blessed Sacrament was exposed throughout the day in the Borgia Chapel.

The day of election began with an early morning Mass of the Holy Spirit at which Father Vicar presided and preached, assisted at the altar by Lisbert D'Souza (BOM) and Tomasz Kot (PMA), the most senior and most junior Regional Assistants. At the end of the Eucharist the Electors processed to aula, where they sang the *Veni Creator Spiritus*. Lisbert D'Souza gave a twenty-minute exhortation that reminded the Electors of key texts from the Scriptures and the *Constitutions*. In accordance with *Formula* 75, all prayed silently for the remainder of the hour.

After fulfilling the prescriptions of the *Formula*, Arturo Marcelino Sosa Abascal (VEN), Delegate for the Roman Houses, was elected the 31st Superior General of the Society of Jesus. Immediately after the Vicar read the decree that certified the election, Antonio Spadaro (ITA) informed the Holy Father. Then the communications team entered the aula to record the General's profession of faith, the traditional reverence accorded the new General, and the congratulations of all the Jesuits present at the Curia. A prayer service that included the *Te Deum* then took place in the Borgia Chapel. The following morning Father Sosa presided at a Mass of Thanksgiving at the Church of the Gesù. He called those present not only to the "audacity of the improbable" mentioned by Father Cadoré at the opening Mass but also to the "audacity of the impossible," because as the Angel Gabriel announced to Mary, "Nothing is impossible for God."

6. The Business Phase of General Congregation 36

At the first session of the business phase of General Congregation 36, the Electors formally welcomed three Members whom Father Nicolás had appointed: Michael J. Garanzini (UCS, Secretary for Higher Education), José Alberto Mesa (COL, Secretary for Education), and Thomas W. Smolich (CFN, Director of the Jesuit Refugee Service). Father Secretary Torres noted that the Conference of

Latin America needed to elect a substitute for the Deputation on the State of the Society to replace Father Sosa.

Father Sosa made a few initial remarks about governance and raised some preliminary questions about which he wanted to receive feedback from the members of the Congregation. He also announced that in accordance with *FCG* 88, §7 Father Nicolás had chosen to leave the Congregation so that he could spend some time in Spain before assuming a new assignment in the Philippines Province.

The Congregation spent 23 days dealing with an array of different issues in a number of different settings. Small group discussions provided the Congregation members a particularly important opportunity to deepen their comprehension and appreciation of one another's experience and thoughts about a wide range of topics. Conference meetings clarified regional perspectives. Plenary sessions provided a forum for developing a universal viewpoint. Redactors worked assiduously to provide invaluable and nuanced summaries to further the Congregation's work. The authors and editors of draft proposals worked long hours honing texts to meet the requirements of the Congregation.

Father General frequently announced his appointment of new Provincials, many of whom were in the aula. He also announced his intention to name Antoine Kerhuel (GAL) as Secretary of the Society. In thanking Ignacio Echarte (ESP) for his years of service in Rome as Secretary and Delegate for the Roman Houses, Father Sosa indicated that the transition to the new Secretary would take place early in 2017.

In addition, preparing *ternae* for the selection of Regional Assistants and electing Assistants *ad providentiam* and the Admonitor required the personal reflection, dialogue, careful attention, and the active participation of all the members of the Congregation. Based on the consultation Father Sosa received from the Members of Assistancies and from the General Councilors, on Monday, 31 October, Father Sosa named the first members of his team. As Regional Assistants he chose Victor Assouad (EOC), Joaquín Barrero Díaz (EMR), Vernon D'Cunha (ASM), Lisbert D'Souza (ASM), Daniel P. Huang (ASP), Tomasz Kot (ECO), Douglas Marcouiller (CUS), Fratern Masawe (AFR), Claudio Paul (ALM), and Gabriel Ignacio Rodríguez (ALS). He also named José Magadia (PHI) as General Councilor for Formation and John Dardis (HIB) as General Councilor for Discernment and Apostolic Planning.

After four days of private conversations and information gathering, on Friday, 4 November, the Congregation elected the Assistants *ad providentiam*: John Dardis, Vernon D'Cunha, Douglas Marcouiller, and Fratern Masawe. The Congregation then determined that Douglas Marcouiller would serve as Admonitor for the General.

7. The Papal Visit

Perhaps the single most important day of the business phase of the Congregation was the visit of Pope Francis on Monday, 24 October. The papal recommendation to ask insistently for consolation, to let ourselves be moved by our Crucified Lord in His person and in His people, and to act in the Good Spirit as men of discernment who think with the Church noticeably resonated in the heads and hearts of all those present in the aula that morning. During the period of questions and answers that followed the Holy Father's prepared remarks, his personal witness to the importance of consolation, compassion, and discernment in serving the Lord and His Church was profoundly moving. The fraternal message and closeness of the Pope inspired and encouraged the Congregation as its work continued.

8. Companions in a Mission of Reconciliation and Justice

The Commission on Jesuit Life and Mission attempted to examine the processes, causes, and consequences that link Jesuit community life with the apostolic realities of ecology, migration, fundamentalism, and ministry among indigenous peoples. They examined in detail more than 75 postulates and six themes submitted by the Provinces. The commission and the Congregation took this challenge seriously in considering six drafts and 173 proposed amendments before approving the final version of the decree, *Companions in a Mission of Reconciliation and Justice.*

Recalling the experience of the First Companions in Venice as they discerned what to do when political conditions thwarted them from going to Jerusalem, the Congregation emphasized that today's Jesuit communities require the characteristics that make them capable of communal apostolic discernment. Members of such communities, on fire with passion for witnessing the Gospel, can participate in the mission of Christ the Reconciler, especially as St. Paul articulates it in 2 Cor. 5:18. Thus, all Jesuit ministerial activities and all Jesuit ministries will have renewed fervor for reconciliation with God, humanity, and creation.

9. Renewed Governance for Renewed Mission

The Commission on Renewed Governance for Renewed Mission based its work on the 68 postulates and five themes that the Province Congregations submitted by the time it began its work as well as other postulates that arrived before the end of the General Congregation. The commission asked for assistance from a number of task forces, working groups, and individuals who all provided important input for deliberation. The resulting document *Renewed Governance for Renewed Mission* emphasized the centrality of the Society's mission for any structure, procedure, or element of governance. Three key features of governance in the Society today are discernment, collaboration, and networking. Therefore, establishing the conditions and means for developing these features is important at each level of the Society's organization. The decree makes six specific recommendations to Father General and those who work with him in Rome, two recommendations to the Conferences of Major Superiors, three to Major Superiors in the Provinces and Regions, and two to local Superiors.

In addition, the Congregation entrusted three important matters to Father General: renewal of the organization and structures of the interprovincial houses in Rome (*Domus Interprovinciales Romanae*); promoting within the Society and its ministries a consistent culture of protection and safety of minors; and a revision of the *Formulae* for a Provincial Congregation, a General Congregation, a Congregation of Procurators, and a Congregation to elect a Vicar General.

Finally, GC 36 modified *Complementary Norms* 362 and 396 to provide greater precision in language and to clarify practice; it also supplied explanatory notes for *Constitutions* 701 and 704 to bring them into conformity with the current *Code of Canon Law*.

10. Witnesses of Friendship and Reconciliation

The last decree taken up by the General Congregation was a letter to and prayer for Jesuits living in zones of war and conflict. John Dardis (HIB), Jean-Baptiste Ganza Gasanana (RWB), and Dany Younès (PRO) comprised a special commission that composed a document that summarized well the sentiments and desires of the Congregation about expressing solidarity with those who witness to the Prince of Peace in places of severe conflict.

11. Conclusion of General Congregation 36

On 11 November, the members determined that they would finish all their business the following day.

Therefore, a prayerful evaluation of the entire proceedings of the Congregation began. Reflections in Assistancy groups, small groups, and individually—ably organized by Pablo José Alonso Vicente (ESP), Mark A. Ravizza (CFN), and Antonio F. Moreno (PHI)—enabled the members to give thanks for the blessings of the past two years and to make suggestions about what might be improved for future Congregations.

Although any member could have intervened to ask that the Congregation might attend to any necessary changes in the decrees, no one did so. Therefore, after an extended period for morning prayer on the last morning, the Congregation determined that Father General and the Assistants *ad providentiam* could approve the final *Acta* of the Congregation. The Congregation also determined that Father General could make any necessary corrections to the decrees "according to the mind of the Congregation" and "after consultation with deliberative vote with those Fathers of the General Curia who have the right to by reason of their office to attend a General Congregation" (*FCG* 140, §4, 2°). Father General and Father Torres then thanked the members of the Congregation and all those whose prayers and labors helped the proceedings in many different ways. Finally, the members declared their work complete and voted to adjourn permanently before singing the *Te Deum* in thanksgiving for the many blessings received.

The members of the Congregation, the Jesuits of Rome, and many friends of the Society of Jesus gathered at the Church of Sant'Ignazio at 16:00 to celebrate a Eucharist of Thanksgiving and to sing the *Te Deum* together. Father General's homily emphasized discernment in solidarity with the others, especially the poor, as the Society goes forth to proclaim the Gospel everywhere. Texts in Latin, Italian, Spanish, English, Polish, Portuguese, Romanian, Japanese, French, Sinhalese and Arabic, as well as special Congolese and Indian rituals, emphasized the universality of the Church. A reception followed at the Gregorian University.

Thus, the 36th General Congregation of the Society of Jesus ended on 12 November 2016 after 35 working days.

DECREE 1

Companions in a Mission of Reconciliation and Justice

*All this is from God, who reconciled us to himself through Christ,
and has given us the ministry of reconciliation.* (2 Cor. 5:18)

1. The Society of Jesus has always sought to know and to follow God's will for
us. This Congregation takes up that task again. We do so from the heart of the
Church, but gazing upon the world "that has been groaning in labor pains until
now."[1] On the one hand, we see the vibrancy of youth, yearning to better their
lives. We see people enjoying the beauty of creation. We see the many ways in
which people use their gifts for the sake of others. And yet, our world faces so
many needs today, so many challenges. We have images in our minds of people
humiliated, struck by violence, excluded from society, and on the margins. The
earth bears the weight of the damage human beings have wrought. Hope itself
seems threatened; in place of hope, we find fear and anger.

2. Pope Francis reminds us that "we are faced not with two separate crises,
one environmental and the other social, but rather with one complex crisis
which is both social and environmental."[2] This one crisis that underlies both
the social and environmental crises arises from the way in which human
beings use—and abuse—the peoples and goods of the earth. This crisis has
deep spiritual roots; it saps the hope and joy that God proclaims and offers
through the Gospel, affecting even the Church and the Society of Jesus.

3. Yet, looking at reality with the eyes of faith, with a vision trained by the *Contemplatio,*[3] we know that God labors in the world. We recognize the signs of
God's work, of the great ministry of reconciliation God has begun in Christ,
fulfilled in the Kingdom of justice, peace, and the integrity of creation. GC
35 recognized this mission.[4] The letter of Father General Adolfo Nicolás
on reconciliation[5] and the teaching of Pope Francis[6] have given this vision

---

[1] Rom. 8:22.

[2] *Laudato si'*, 139.

[3] "The Contemplation to Attain Love," in *Spiritual Exercises*, 236.

[4] Cf. GC 35, D. 3, "Challenges to Our Mission Today." In doing so, GC 35
built upon the message of GC 32, D. 4, n. 2. "The mission of the Society of Jesus today
is the service of faith, of which the promotion of justice is an absolute requirement. For
reconciliation with God demands the reconciliation of people with one another."

[5] Father Adolfo Nicolás, "Reply to *Ex Officio* Letters 2014," *Acta Romana Societatis Iesu* XXV (2014): 1032–1038.

[6] Cf. *Evangelii gaudium*, 226–230, 239–258, and *Misericordiae vultus.*

greater depth, placing faith, justice, and solidarity with the poor and the excluded as central elements of the mission of reconciliation. Rather than ask what we should do, we seek to understand how God invites us—and so many people of good will—to share in that great work. Alone, we find ourselves humbled and weak, sinners. With the Psalmist, we cry out, "Show us, O Lord, your mercy, and grant us your salvation."[7] But we experience joy in knowing ourselves as sinners who, in God's mercy, are called to be companions of Jesus and "co-workers with God."[8]

4. We are not the first to seek clarity concerning God's call. The meeting of the First Companions in Venice[9] is a powerful image, an important step in the formation of the Society. There, the companions confronted the frustration of their plans to go to the Holy Land. This drove them to a deeper discernment of the Lord's call. Where was the Spirit drawing them? As they discerned new direction for their lives, they held fast to what they had already found to be life-giving: sharing their lives together as friends in the Lord; living very close to the lives of the poor; and preaching the Gospel with joy.

5. They were priests, both learned and poor. For the First Companions, life and mission, rooted in a discerning community, were profoundly inter-related. We Jesuits today are called to live in the same way, as priests, brothers, and those in formation who all share the same mission. As we reflect and pray on each of these elements, we do so knowing the intimate unity of mission, life, and discerning community, all afire with the love of Christ.

6. This Congregation finds consolation and joy in returning to these roots, this integral vision of who we are, as well as in the knowledge that there are many others who, like us, hear the call to labor with Christ. We return to those roots now, first to a discerning community, then to our life in faith, and finally to the mission that flows from both. The poverty of life and proximity to the poor of the First Companions in Venice must mark our lives too,[10] that poverty that engenders creativity and protects us from what limits our availability to respond to God's call. Such poverty of life constantly calls us to reflect on how we can live more simply with less. We pray too to enter ever more fully into that great mystical tradition that our First Fathers bequeathed to us, ever a grace, ever a challenge. Finally, we insistently ask for the grace to know how we can share in the great ministry

---

[7] Ps. 85:8.

[8] 1 Cor. 3:9.

[9] *Autobiography,* 93–95.

[10] *CN,* 143, 159–160. Our poverty is for us *madre* (*Constitutions,* 287) and *muro* (*Constitutions,* 553).

of reconciliation, knowing that as Pope Francis reminds us, our response remains always incomplete.[11]

A Discerning Community with Open Horizons

7. During their time in Venice, the companions were not always together; they were dispersed in order to fulfill many tasks. Nevertheless, it was at that time that they shared the experience of constituting a single group, united in following Christ, in the midst of the diversity of their activities. We Jesuits today are also engaged in a great variety of apostolates, which often demand specialization and a great deal of energy. If, however, we forget that we are one body, bound together in and with Christ,[12] we lose our identity as Jesuits and our ability to bear witness to the Gospel. It is our union with one another in Christ that testifies to the Good News more powerfully than our competences and abilities.

8. Thus, each of us should constantly desire that our own apostolic work develop, be stimulated, and helped to bear fruit, through the encouragement of our brothers. We always receive our mission from God in the Church, through our Major Superiors and local Superiors, in the practice of Jesuit obedience, which includes our personal discernment.[13] If, however, our mission is not supported by the body of the Society, it risks withering. In our individualistic and competitive age, we should remember that the community plays a very special role since it is a privileged place of apostolic discernment.

9. The Jesuit community is a concrete space in which we live as friends in the Lord. This life together is always at the service of mission, but because these fraternal bonds proclaim the Gospel, it is itself a mission.[14]

10. In our Jesuit community life, we should leave room for encounter and sharing. This disposition helps the community become a space of truth, joy, creativity, pardon, and of seeking the will of God. Thus, community can become a place of discernment.

11. Communal discernment requires that each of us develop some basic characteristics and attitudes: availability, mobility, humility, freedom, the ability to accompany others, patience, and a willingness to listen respectfully so that we may speak the truth to each other.

---

[11] Interview with Pope Francis, *Civiltà Cattolica* 2013 III: 449–477.

[12] *Constitutions*, 813.

[13] GC 35, D. 4.

[14] GC 35, D. 2, 19, and D. 3, 41, and Father Peter-Hans Kolvenbach, "On Community Life," nn. 2 and 10, *Acta Romana Societatis Iesu* XXII (1998): 279–280, 288. Cf. *CN*, 314–330.

12. An essential tool that can animate apostolic communal discernment is spiritual conversation. Spiritual conversation involves an exchange marked by active and receptive listening and a desire to speak of that which touches us most deeply. It tries to take account of spiritual movements, individual and communal, with the objective of choosing the path of consolation that fortifies our faith, hope, and love. Spiritual conversation creates an atmosphere of trust and welcome for ourselves and others. We ought not to deprive ourselves of such conversation in the community and in all other occasions for decision-making in the Society.

13. In our world that knows too much division, we ask God to help our communities become "homes" for the Reign of God. We hear the call to overcome what can separate us from one another. Simplicity of life and openness of heart foster such mutual concern. Moreover, living together as friends in the Lord nurtures the vocations of our men in formation and can inspire men to enter the Society.

14. Of course, this disposition to attend to the Spirit in our relationships must include those with whom we work. Often they teach us this openness to the Spirit. Important discernments concerning mission are often enriched by their voices and their commitment.

15. It is critical to emphasize the continuing relevance of the real closeness of the First Companions to the poor. The poor challenge us to return constantly to what is essential to the Gospel, to what really gives life, and to recognize that which merely burdens us. As Pope Francis reminds us: we are called to find Christ in the poor, to lend our voice to their causes, but also to be their friends, to listen to them, to understand them, and to embrace the mysterious wisdom that God wishes to share with us through them.[15] Such an attitude runs counter to the usual way of the world, in which, as Qoheleth says, "the poor man's wisdom is despised, and his words are not heeded."[16] With the poor, we can learn what hope and courage mean.

16. In our communities and apostolates, we hear the call to rediscover hospitality to strangers, to the young, to the poor, and to those who are persecuted. Christ himself teaches us this hospitality.

Men on Fire with Passion for the Gospel

17. Our First Fathers entered into such a rich discernment of God's call together because they had experienced the grace of Christ that set them free. Pope Francis urges us to pray insistently for this consolation that Christ desires

---

[15] See *Evangelii gaudium,* n. 198.
[16] Ecclesiastes 9:16.

to give.[17] Reconciliation with God is first and foremost a call to a profound conversion, for each Jesuit, and for all of us.

18. The question that confronts the Society today is why the Exercises do not change us as deeply as we would hope. What elements in our lives, works, or lifestyles hinder our ability to let God's gracious mercy transform us? This Congregation is deeply convinced that God is calling the entire Society to a profound spiritual renewal. Ignatius reminds us that each Jesuit must "take care, as long as he lives, first of all to keep before his eyes God."[18] Thus, all the means that unite us directly with God should be more than ever prized and practiced: the *Spiritual Exercises*, daily prayer, the Eucharist and the Sacrament of Reconciliation, spiritual direction, and the Examen.[19] We need to appropriate ever more fully the gift of the *Exercises* that we share with so many, especially the Ignatian family,[20] and the *Constitutions* that animate our Society. In a world losing its sense of God, we should seek to be more deeply united with Christ in the mysteries of his life. Through the *Exercises*, we acquire the style of Jesus, his feelings, his choices.

19. At the heart of Ignatian spirituality is the transforming encounter with the mercy of God in Christ that moves us to a generous personal response. The experience of the merciful gaze of God on our weakness and sinfulness humbles us and fills us with gratitude, helping us to become compassionate ministers to all.[21] Filled with the fire of Christ's mercy, we can inflame those we meet. This foundational experience of God's mercy has always been the source of the apostolic audacity that has marked the Society and which we must preserve.

20. "Mercy," Pope Francis reminds us, "is not an abstraction but a lifestyle consisting in concrete gestures rather than mere words."[22] For us Jesuits, compassion is action, an action discerned together. Yet we know that there is no authentic familiarity with God if we do not allow ourselves to be moved to compassion and action by an encounter with the Christ who is revealed in the suffering, vulnerable faces of people, indeed in the suffering of creation.[23]

On Mission with Christ the Reconciler

21. In preparation for the 36th General Congregation, Father General Adolfo Nicolás invited the Society to enter into a process of seeking to hear "the call of the Eternal King, and to discern the three most important calls that

---

[17] Address of Pope Francis to GC 36, 24 October 2016.
[18] *Formula of the Institute* (1550), 1.
[19] *Constitutions*, 813.
[20] GC 35, D 6, n. 29.
[21] Address of Pope Francis to GC 36, 24 October 2016.
[22] Ibid.
[23] Cf. Matthew 25: 31–46.

the Lord makes to the whole Society today."[24] Our Provinces and Regions, through the Province and Regional Congregations, responded to this invitation. The call to share God's work of reconciliation in our broken world emerged often and powerfully. What GC 35 had identified as three dimensions of this ministry of reconciliation,[25] namely, reconciliation with God, with one another, and with creation, assumed a new urgency. This reconciliation is always a work of justice, a justice discerned and enacted in local communities and contexts. The Cross of Christ and our sharing in it are also at the center of God's work of reconciliation. This mission can lead to conflict and death, as we have witnessed in the lives of many of our brothers. While we speak of three forms of reconciliation, all three are, in reality, one work of God, interconnected and inseparable.

1st Call—Reconciliation with God

22. Reconciliation with God roots us in gratitude and opens us to joy, if we allow it. Pope Francis writes, "The joy of the Gospel fills the hearts and lives of all who encounter Jesus. [...] With Christ, joy is constantly born anew."[26] Announcing and sharing the Gospel continues to be the reason for the Society's existence and mission: that Jesus Christ be known, that he be loved in return, and that Christ's love be a source of life for all. He always remains the source of the joy and hope we offer to others. Thus, the Society must respond more decisively to the Church's call for a new evangelization, giving special emphasis to ministry to and with the young and with families.

23. A special gift Jesuits and the Ignatian family have to offer to the Church and her mission of evangelization is Ignatian spirituality, which facilitates the experience of God and can therefore greatly help the process of personal and communal conversion. Pope Francis constantly affirms that discernment should play a special role, in the family, among youth, in vocation promotion, and in the formation of clergy.[27] Christian life is more and more personalized through discernment.

24. Proclaiming the Gospel takes place in many different contexts: a) Secularization is a major challenge for many cultures, calling for creativity particularly in attracting and initiating younger generations into the Christian faith. b) In an increasingly pluralistic world, inter-religious dialogue in all its forms remains a necessity, one that is not always easy and that risks misunderstanding. c) In many parts of the world, the Society is called to respond

---

[24] Father Adolfo Nicolás, "Letter Convoking General Congregation 36," *Acta Romana Societatis Iesu* XXV (2014): 1096.
[25] GC 35, D. 3.
[26] *Evangelii gaudium*, 1.
[27] *Amoris laetitia*, 296–306.

to the challenge of believers abandoning the Church in the search for personal meaning and spirituality. d) Jesuits must continue to give importance to theological and scriptural studies by which we help people deepen their understanding of the Gospel in their diverse cultural contexts, with their hopes and their challenges. These studies should involve accompanying people from the depth of their spiritual traditions.

2nd Call—Reconciliation within Humanity

25. Throughout our preparation for this Congregation as a universal body with a universal mission,[28] we heard accounts of the shocking forms of suffering and injustice that millions of our brothers and sisters endure. Reflecting on these, we hear Christ summon us anew to a ministry of justice and peace, serving the poor and the excluded, and helping build peace. Among these various forms of suffering, three have appeared with consistency from many of our Provinces and Regions:

   a. [26.] The displacement of peoples (refugees, migrants, and internally displaced peoples): In the face of attitudes hostile to these displaced persons, our faith invites the Society to promote everywhere a more generous culture of hospitality. The Congregation recognizes the necessity of promoting the international articulation of our service to migrants and refugees, finding ways of collaboration with JRS.

   b. [27.] The injustices and inequalities experienced by marginalized peoples: Along with an enormous growth of wealth and power in the world comes an enormous and continuing growth of inequality. The present dominant models of development leave millions of people, especially the young and the vulnerable, without opportunities for integration into society. Indigenous peoples and communities, like the Dalits and tribals in South Asia, represent a paradigmatic case of these groups. In many parts of the world, women especially experience such injustice. We are called to support these communities in their struggles, recognizing that we have much to learn from their values and their courage. The defense and promotion of human rights and integral ecology is an ethical horizon that we share with many other people of good will, who are also seeking to respond to this call.

   c. [28.] Fundamentalism, intolerance, and ethnic-religious-political conflicts as a source of violence: In many societies, there is an increased level of conflict and polarization, which often gives rise to violence that is all the more appalling because it is motivated and justified by distorted religious convictions. In such situations, Jesuits, along with all who seek the common

---

[28] GC 35, D. 2, n. 20.

good, are called to contribute from their religious-spiritual traditions towards the building of peace, on local and global levels.

3rd Call—Reconciliation with Creation

29. Pope Francis has emphasized the fundamental connection between the environmental crisis and the social crisis in which we live today.[29] Poverty, social exclusion, and marginalization are linked with environmental degradation. These are not separate crises but one crisis that is a symptom of something much deeper: the flawed way societies and economies are organized. The current economic system with its predatory orientation discards natural resources as well as people.[30] For this reason, Pope Francis insists that the only adequate solution must be a radical one. The direction of development must be altered if it is to be sustainable. We Jesuits are called to help heal a broken world,[31] promoting a new way of producing and consuming, which puts God's creation at the center.

30. The multifaceted challenge of caring for our common home calls for a multifaceted response from the Society. We begin by changing our personal and community lifestyles, adopting behavior coherent with our desire for reconciliation with creation. We must accompany and remain close to the most vulnerable. Our theologians, philosophers, and other intellectuals and experts should contribute to the rigorous analysis of the roots of and solutions to the crisis. Jesuit commitment in regions like the Amazon and the Congo Basin, environmental reserves that are essential for the future of humanity, should be supported. We should manage our financial investments responsibly. And we cannot forget to celebrate creation, to give thanks for "so much good we have received."[32]

Toward the Renewal of Our Apostolic Life

31. All our ministries should seek to build bridges, to foster peace.[33] To do this, we must enter into a deeper understanding of the mystery of evil in the world and the transforming power of the merciful gaze of God who labors to create of humanity one reconciled, peaceful family. With Christ, we are called to closeness with all of crucified humanity. With the poor, we can contribute to creating one human family through the struggle for justice. Those who

---

[29] *Laudato si'*, 139.

[30] "Justice in the Global Economy: Building Sustainable and Inclusive Communities," *Promotio iustitiae* 121.

[31] "Healing a Broken World," *Promotio iustitiae* 106.

[32] *Spiritual Exercises*, 233.

[33] *Formula of the Institute* (1550) 1: "He should show himself ready to reconcile the estranged."

have all the necessities of life and live far from poverty also need the message of hope and reconciliation, which frees them from fear of migrants and refugees, the excluded and those who are different, and that opens them to hospitality and to making peace with enemies.

32. The Congregation calls the entire Society to a renewal of our apostolic life founded on hope. We need more than ever to bring a message of hope, born of consolation from our encounter with the Risen Lord. This renewal focused on hope includes all our diverse apostolates.

33. We do not want to propose a simplistic or superficial hope. Rather, our contribution, as Father Adolfo Nicolás always insisted, should be characterized by depth: a depth of interiority and "a depth of reflection that allows us to understand reality more deeply and thus to serve more effectively."[34] To this end, Jesuits in formation should receive solid intellectual preparation and be helped to grow in personal integration.

34. Our educational apostolates at all levels, and our centers for communication and social research, should help form men and women committed to reconciliation and able to confront obstacles to reconciliation and propose solutions. The intellectual apostolate should be strengthened to help in the transformation of our cultures and societies.

35. Because of the magnitude and interconnectedness of the challenges we face, it is important to support and encourage the growing collaboration among Jesuits and Jesuit apostolates through networks. International and intersectoral networks are an opportunity to strengthen our identity, as we share our capacities and local engagements in order together to serve a universal mission.

36. Collaboration with others is the only way the Society of Jesus can fulfill the mission entrusted to her. This partnership in mission includes those with whom we share Christian faith, those who belong to different religions, and women and men of good will, who, like us, desire to collaborate with Christ's reconciling work. In the words of Father General Arturo Sosa, Jesuits are "called to the mission of Jesus Christ, that does not belong to us exclusively, but that we share with so many men and women consecrated to the service of others."[35]

37. In all we do, we want to heed Pope Francis, who has urged us to promote dynamics of personal and social transformation. "What we need is to give

---

[34] Father Adolfo Nicolás, "Letter on Intellectual Formation," *Acta Romana Societatis Iesu* XXV (2014): 926.

[35] Homily of Father General Arturo Sosa, 15 October 2016.

priority to actions which generate new processes in society."[36] Prayerful discernment ought to be our habitual way of drawing closer to reality when we want to transform it.

38. Aware of the urgency of the present moment and of the need to involve all the Society and its apostolates in responding to these calls, this Congregation asks Father General, working closely with the Conferences and Provinces, to develop clear goals and guidelines for our apostolic life today.

Conclusion

39. From Venice, Ignatius and his companions journeyed to Rome, there to give shape to the one apostolic body of the Society, and to launch an extraordinary missionary activity. They did so under the Roman Pontiff, who confirmed their charism. This Congregation has experienced a similar grace of confirmation, encouragement and mission from Pope Francis. The Holy Father emphasized that we should not be satisfied with the *status quo* of our ministries. He called us again to the *magis*, "that *plus*" that led "Ignatius to begin processes, to follow them through, and to evaluate their real impact on the lives of persons."[37]

40. In faith, we know that, amidst the difficulties and challenges of our time, God never ceases to labor for the salvation of all people, indeed of all creation. We believe that God continues his work of "reconciling the world to himself in Christ."[38] We hear the urgent summons to join the Lord in caring for the neediest and to extend God's mercy to where injustice, suffering or despair seem to thwart the divine plan. We pray for the courage and the freedom "to dare the audacity of the 'improbable,'" as we respond to God's call "with the humility of those who know that, in this service where the human engages all his energy, 'everything depends on God.'"[39] "Now is the acceptable time! Now is the day of salvation!"[40]

---

[36] *Evangelii gaudium*, 223.

[37] Address of Pope Francis to GC 36, 24 October 2016. Cf. *Evangelii gaudium*, 223: "Giving priority to time means being concerned about initiating processes rather than possessing spaces."

[38] 2 Cor. 5:19.

[39] Homily of Rev. Bruno Cadoré, O.P., at the opening of GC 36.

[40] 2 Cor. 6:2.

DECREE 2

Renewed Governance for a Renewed Mission

Introduction

1. Apostolic mission lies at the very heart of the Society. From its earliest days, discernment has guided the development of governance to better serve and support the Society's mission, the *Missio Dei*. Governance in the Society is personal, spiritual, and apostolic. Each General Congregation is a source of inspiration that guides the development of governance in changing circumstances and the care for the persons engaged in this mission in ways most appropriate to the times.

2. GC 35 gave helpful recommendations to guide the Society's governance, many of which have been implemented. Reviewing progress, GC 36 points to several areas that need further attention and clarification. First, GC 36 identifies important features relevant to our way of proceeding today that we wish to encourage. Second, this Congregation acknowledges the ways in which renewal of governance has already been undertaken at diverse levels in the Society since GC 35. Third, GC 36 makes clarifications and recommendations for ongoing apostolic discernment and planning.

Ways of Proceeding Suited to Our Times

3. Discernment, collaboration and networking offer three important perspectives on our contemporary way of proceeding. As the Society of Jesus is an "international and multicultural body" in a complex, "fragmented and divided world,"[1] attention to these perspectives helps to streamline governance and make it more flexible and apostolically effective.

4. ***Discernment:*** Discernment, a precious gift of Ignatius, is integral to our personal and corporate apostolic life. It begins in contemplation of God at work in our world and allows us to draw more fruit in joining our efforts to God's designs. Discernment is what "roots us in the Church in which the Spirit works and distributes his various gifts for the common good."[2] Discernment serves as the foundation for decision-making by the proper authority in our way of proceeding. In preparing for this Congregation we already have an experience of discernment that began in Provinces and Regions and helped us to name both significant challenges to our mission today and our

---

[1] GC 35, D. 3, n. 43.
[2] Address of Pope Francis to GC 36, 24 October 2016.

responses to the Good News of Jesus.[3] This discernment process offers the spiritual base that enables our apostolic planning.

5. Given the magnitude and complexity of contemporary challenges to the mission, and the declining numbers in our least Society, discernment is more than ever critical for apostolic effectiveness.[4] Consistent and participative discernment is our way of ensuring that ongoing apostolic planning, including implementation, monitoring, and evaluation, is an integral element in all Jesuit ministry. Given the crisis of authority in contemporary culture (family life, education, politics, religion), the practice of discernment is a gift that we can offer to others. By living discernment, we can impart its practice to others. Sharing in discernment leads to a shared vision. Forming collaborators for mission means first that we be formed for discernment.

6. ***Collaboration:*** GC 35 stated that "collaboration in mission [...] expresses our true identity as members of the Church, the complementarity of our diverse calls to holiness, our mutual responsibility for the mission of Christ, our desire to join people of good will in the service of the human family, and the coming of the Kingdom of God."[5] GC 34 had already asked that "all those engaged in the work should exercise coresponsibility and be engaged in discernment and participative decision making where it is appropriate."[6] GC 36 recognizes the decisive role of our partners in the vitality of the Society's mission today and expresses its gratitude to all those who contribute to and play significant roles in Jesuit ministry. That mission is deepened and ministry is extended by collaboration among all with whom we work, especially those inspired by the Ignatian call.

7. Noting remarkable progress in collaboration across the Society, obstacles remain. The challenges may be found in our own lack of imagination and courage, or they may come from inhibitions arising from our social contexts or even from local clerical practice. A particular difficulty can be the lack of genuine collaboration among Jesuits—individuals, institutions, communities, Provinces, and Conferences. Inclusive discernment and ongoing planning and evaluation of our efforts to go beyond the obstacles is required in order to mainstream the participation of mission partners further in various levels of the Society's apostolic activities and governance. It is also important to discern to which projects, initiatives, or activities

---

[3] See Father Adolfo Nicolás, "GC 36: The Call of the Eternal King; A Meditation" (2015/15: 3 October 2015).

[4] See Father Adolfo Nicolás, "CP70: *De statu S.J.,*" *Acta Romana Societatis Iesu* XXV, 2 (2012): 535.

[5] GC 35, D. 6, n. 30.

[6] GC 34, D. 13, n. 13.

carried out by others, we could offer our support, whether human, technical, intellectual, or financial.

8. ***Networking:*** Collaboration naturally leads to cooperation through networks. New technologies of communication open up forms of organization that facilitate collaboration. They make it possible to mobilize human and material resources in support of mission, and to go beyond national borders and the boundaries of Provinces and Regions. Often mentioned in our recent Congregation documents, networking builds on a shared vision and requires a culture of generosity, openness to work with others and a desire to celebrate successes. Networks also depend on persons able to provide vision and leadership for collaborative mission. When properly conceived, networking provides a healthy balance between authority and local initiative. It strengthens local capacity and encourages subsidiarity while assuring a unified sense of mission from a central authority. Local views are more readily and speedily heard.

9. Governing bodies in the Society are already encouraging networks. Depending upon their scope and scale, Provincials, Conferences, and the General Curia actively facilitate, foster, accompany, and evaluate international and intersectoral networks. In Jesuit networks we find the intersection between the creativity and initiative that occur in networking and the authority that gives the mission. Networks engage the "horizontal" and the "vertical" dimensions of our ministries and governance. Networking also reflects a contemporary move towards greater synodality as promoted by Vatican II.

Review of Steps Taken since GC 35

10. Decree 5 of GC 35, "Governance at the Service of Universal Mission," expressed the desire that Father General follow up on certain issues expeditiously. This desire was articulated in directives, recommendations, and suggestions. Directives included the comprehensive revision of the *Formulae* for General, Province and Procurators' Congregations, and the instruction to perform a comprehensive review of central governance. Recommendations included the establishment of instruments to promote good governance through regular assessment of superiors and evaluation of apostolic institutions, the evolution of a strategy for improved communications within and beyond the Society, and reflection on provincial and regional structures with a view to adapting them to today's realities. Suggestions for follow-up included the search for ways in which financial resources may be more equitably deployed for solidarity in service of international mission. Another request was that programs for leadership development be undertaken in the Society.

11. Each request received significant attention; time and resources were given to the issues, and substantial progress is evident. GC 36 expresses its deep gratitude to Father Adolfo Nicolás and all who played a role in these efforts.

12. This Congregation identifies three areas for further reflection and action:

   a. The Society should continue to improve its process of discernment, making it always more coherent, that is, better able to identify and respond to challenges at the global level in a way that integrates local, provincial, conference, and central governance. The Society should continue to develop ways at every level to implement, monitor, and evaluate the results of decisions taken.

   b. The breadth and depth of our planning and review processes (for example, the review of central governance and the structures of Conferences) need greater attention and capacity.

   c. Some of the requests of Decree 5 of GC 35 (for example, communications, sharing financial resources, leadership development) have been acted on, but they are still works in progress that need attention.

13. Reflecting on these realities through the perspectives of discernment, collaboration and networking, GC 36 makes the following recommendations.

Recommendations

For Father General and Central Governance

14. GC 36 asks Father General to review the process-initiated by GC 34[7] and continued by Father General Peter-Hans Kolvenbach[8]—to evaluate progress on our current apostolic preferences and, if appropriate, to identify new ones. Discernment of such preferences should include the greatest possible participation of the Society and of those involved with us in our mission. To this end, as indicated by GC 35,[9] Father General and the Council should establish procedures for assessing the Society's complex processes for apostolic planning at all levels and encourage the use of ongoing discernment and planning.

15. GC 36 calls on Father General to carry to term the comprehensive review of the central governance of the Society that was requested by GC 35[10] and initiated by Father Nicolás. In particular, this review should further help situate various governance elements in relation to the General, his Council,

---

[7] GC 34, D. 21, n. 28.

[8] Father Peter-Hans Kolvenbach, "Nos preferénces apostoliques," *Acta Romana Societatis Iesu* XXIII, 1 (2003): 31–36.

[9] GC 35, D. 3, n. 40.

[10] GC 35, D. 5, nn. 9–14.

Regional Assistants, Sectoral Secretaries, Conference Presidents, the Major Superiors, and local Superiors, noting the competencies of each, the complementarity of their roles in serving the Society's mission, and their relationship with the person and governance of Father General. This process should include an evolving communications strategy as noted in Decree 5.[11] For this review, in line with what was proposed by GC 35, Father General is encouraged to "make use of the best professional advice available within and outside the Society."[12]

16. GC 36 requests that Father General study the governance of Jesuit networks and other forms of ministry which extend beyond a Province or Conference. As networking has been promoted to enhance collaboration inside and outside the Society,[13] it is necessary to reflect on how and at what level of governance the Society can exercise its responsibility for Jesuit networks. In the same way, the Society should develop models of governance appropriate to ministries that are global in their mission and service.

17. GC 36 asks Father General to review and evaluate the restructuring of Provinces and Regions that has already taken place, so that what has been learned can be applied to ongoing and future reconfiguration.

18. GC 36 affirms that, keeping in mind our commitment to poverty, various financial strategies, opportunities, and implications must be considered in apostolic planning and decision-making at all levels of Society governance. The Treasurer and other skilled and knowledgeable persons should assist in these processes. In this context, GC 36 requests that Father General implement revisions of the *Statutes on Religious Poverty in the Society of Jesus* and the *Instruction on the Administration of Goods,* with particular attention to the use of contemporary financial instruments and to the norms on sources and uses of the Common Fund.

19. GC 36 calls on Father General to continue the steps taken by Father Nicolás to promote greater solidarity of human, institutional, and financial resources throughout the Society in order to achieve greater apostolic effectiveness. Specifically, the Congregation asks that he:

   a. Continue and bring to fulfillment the Solidarity in Formation process;

   b. Review the goals and operation of FACSI to promote more effectively the universal mission of the Society at the service of those in greater need.

---

[11] GC 35, D. 5, n. 13.
[12] GC 35, D. 5, n. 14.
[13] Cf. GC 34, D. 21, nn. 13–14 and GC 35, D. 6, n. 29.

For Conferences of Major Superiors

20. GC 36 asks that the six Conferences, described by GC 35 as "a significant initiative in the governance structure of the Society,"[14] should undertake a study of their way of proceeding. They should use the guidelines of Decree 5 of GC 35[15] as the foundation for their self-assessment; these self-assessments should be reviewed by Father General. Acknowledging differences in history, context, and styles of decision-making, the self-study should have at least the following four outcomes:

    a. More consistency among the Statutes of the Conferences, particularly in the areas of the binding nature of decisions and the President's decision-making authority in relation to the co-responsibility of Major Superiors.[16]

    b. A process for implementing ongoing apostolic discernment and planning in the Conference that includes the President in the apostolic planning of Provinces and Regions and in facilitating the preparation of Jesuits for international apostolates.

    c. Clarification of their capacity for holding resources for formation and apostolic purposes.

    d. An outline of ways in which the Presidents engage with Father General in discerning and animating the universal mission of the Society and in expanding the horizons of decision-making beyond the confines of Provinces and Conferences.

21. GC 36 calls on Conferences to review implementation of the *Guidelines for the Relationship between the Superior and the Director of Work.*[17] They should take into account the increasing number of lay directors of Jesuit works and adapt the *Guidelines* as needed for the realities of their Conferences. They should further assess the implementation of Decree 6 of GC 35[18] in regard to collaboration with others, and develop and evaluate strategies to promote such collaboration in the Conference. The reduced number of Jesuits, the proliferation of apostolic initiatives of the Society, the increasingly active and welcome participation of partners, and the growing role of lay participation in the Church require further reflection and action in the area of collaboration. Father General should be informed of the strategies and should approve updated Guidelines.

---

[14] GC 35, D. 5, n. 17.

[15] GC 35, D. 5, nn. 17–23.

[16] GC 35, D. 5, n. 20 c.

[17] *Acta Romana Societatis Iesu* XXII, 3 (1998): 383–391.

[18] GC 35, D. 6, n. 29.

For Provincial and Regional Governance

22. GC 36 asks Major Superiors to ensure that apostolic discernment and planning in their Provinces or Regions is consistent with the universal apostolic preferences of the Society and the apostolic discernment and planning of their Conferences, so that the mission preferences of the whole Society are taken into account in the ministries of their Provinces or Regions.[19] Discernment and decisions of Major Superiors about works in their Provinces or Regions must take into account the effects they have on flexibility and availability for the universal mission of the Society, especially in their Conferences. This engagement enhances both the General's capacity to undertake global mission and the Major Superiors' co-responsibility in serving the universal mission of the Society.

23. GC 36 calls on Major Superiors to promote the integration of life and mission of Jesuits at the local level, in the context of decreasing numbers of Jesuits worldwide but increasing involvement of others and growth of apostolic vitality. Major Superiors should insist on the formation of Jesuits who will be able to thrive in this evolving reality. Major Superiors are also encouraged to create and support dynamics which build relationships among Jesuits, enhance collaboration among Jesuits and colleagues, support apostolic animation, and promote initiatives of inter-sectoral collaboration. These initiatives could include meetings among superiors of the same city or area, apostolic networks or platforms, and ministries commissions or other structures of mutual accompaniment. At the same time GC 36 calls on Major Superiors to support processes which give freedom to leave ministries which are no longer sustainable or no longer critical to our mission, and to clarify juridical relationships with ministries which have become Ignatian rather than Jesuit in character.[20]

24. GC 36 requests that Major Superiors ensure that a local Superior's primary responsibility be the animation of the local Jesuit community.[21] Proper training for local Superiors and a manageable workload of apostolic activities are key to the proper implementation of *CN* 351.[22]

For Local Governance

25. GC 35 stated that "the effectiveness of the local Superior is critical to the apostolic vitality of the Jesuit community [...]."[23] The apostolic leadership of the local Superior is today marked by the importance of the promotion of

---

[19] Cf. GC 35, D. 5, n. 20, c. 3.

[20] GC 35, D. 6, nn. 9–14.

[21] Cf. *Complementary Norm,* 351.

[22] GC 35, D. 5, n. 38.

[23] GC 35, D. 5, n. 33.

discernment, collaboration and networking. GC 36 requests that local Superiors exercise their service to communities from these three perspectives so that they promote mission at all levels: local, Province, Conference, and universal.

26. GC 36 invites Superiors and Directors of works, and indeed all Jesuits and partners in mission, to foster deep habits of prayer and discernment as the preludes and accompaniment to ongoing planning, and to foster mutual relationships and collaboration in implementing plans. This means encouraging a spirit of availability and trust among us and with all who serve the *Missio Dei.*

Conclusion: Re-Imagining and Seeking the Greater and More Universal Good

27. If our governance can inspire us to renew our service of mission, with greater commitment to discernment, collaboration, and networking, God's grace can move us closer to its fulfillment.

28. As Pope Francis reminded us, our "way of proceeding" is a process, a journey: "I rather like Ignatius's way of seeing everything—except for what is absolutely essential—as constantly developing, *in fieri* [...]."[24] We draw profit, Pope Francis indicated, from "holding tensions together"[25]: contemplation and action, faith and justice, charism and institutions, community and mission. We are pilgrims. Our path involves facing the creative tensions brought about by the diversity of persons and ministries in the Society. In seeking to progress in following the Lord, the Society must constantly re-imagine and discern how our governance structures can better serve the mission entrusted to us.

---

[24] Address of Pope Francis to GC 36, 24 October 2016.
[25] Ibid.

Appendix: Key Recommendations and Outcomes of GC 35, Decree 5

This appendix is not comprehensive; it is simply a concise evaluation of the requests from GC 35 to the ordinary governance. It shows the importance of accountability and evaluation.

Formulae (nn. 2–6): A comprehensive revision of the *Formulae* for a General Congregation, Province Congregation, and Congregation of Procurators has been completed. Further revision of the *Formulae* should be completed within one year from the end of GC 36.

Comprehensive Review of Central Governance (nn. 7–11): This review was undertaken with several concrete outcomes: job descriptions for Curia staff members, a committee structure for apostolic planning and consultation, and Secretariats for the Service of Faith and Collaboration. The lack of an evaluation process and ongoing concerns about apostolic discernment in central governance would suggest areas for continued focus.

Financial Effectiveness and Equity (n. 12): These processes have been initiated and offer opportunity for significant success.

Communications Strategy (n. 13): Considerable improvements have been made in intra government communications; in an area of constant change, ongoing discernment is needed for more effective communication to the broader world.

Assessment Instruments (n. 15): Practica quaedam was updated; new instruments to review implementation and accountability were developed; new evaluations for final vows were implemented.

Conferences (nn. 17–23): GC 35 provided an overview of the structure, the role of the Conference President, and decision-making processes for this still-evolving dimension of the Society's governance. N. 18. c. 2 asked Conferences to adapt their Statutes in light of GC 35, a task accomplished. However, the concerns brought to GC 36 about Conferences suggest the need for ongoing reflection and evaluation.

Province Structures (nn. 24–28): In n. 26, GC 35 mandated a commission to reflect on Provinces and province structures with the goal of providing guidance for the establishment, reconfiguration and suppression of Provinces and Regions. The commission's work has facilitated significant progress in the evolving structures of Provinces and Regions worldwide.

Apostolic Works (n. 29): Instruments to evaluate apostolic institutions in function of their contribution to mission have been developed.

Training for Leadership (nn. 30–32): Noteworthy steps forward have been made principally through programs initiated by Conferences for Jesuits and lay colleagues.

Local Superiors (nn. 33–39): These paragraphs outline principles, challenges, and recommendations for local leadership. *Ex officio* letters and other sources suggest that, due to other responsibilities, many local superiors find it difficult to make the animation of the local community their primary responsibility (n. 38).

Superiors and Directors of Works (nn. 40–42): The relationship between the Superior and Director of work(s) can be a neuralgic issue, especially in places where lay leadership of Jesuit ministries is not yet common. N. 40 directed adaptation of the *Guidelines for the Relationship between the Superior and the Director of Work* to the local context in dialogue with the Major Superior.

OTHER DOCUMENTS

Witnesses of Friendship and Reconciliation: A Message and a Prayer for Jesuits Living in Zones of War and Conflict

Blessed be the God and Father of our Lord Jesus Christ, the Father of mercies and the God of all consolation, who consoles us in all our affliction, so that we may be able to console those who are in any affliction with the consolation with which we ourselves are consoled by God. [...] Our hope for you is unshaken; for we know that as you share in our sufferings, so also you share in our consolation. (2 Cor. 1: 3–4, 7)

Since the last General Congregation, we have seen situations of heart-breaking conflict in many parts of the world. The sad litany includes Syria and South Sudan, Colombia, and the Great Lakes region of Africa, the Central African Republic, Afghanistan, Ukraine, Iraq, and so many other places. There has been devastating loss of life and massive displacement of peoples. These conflicts have a global reach. Those who serve at the frontline have been especially affected. In solidarity and with deep affection, we write this message to our fellow Jesuits living and working in situations of violence and war.

Dear Companions and Friends in the Lord,

We, the Jesuits gathered at GC 36, greet and support you, our fellow Jesuits, who serve at the frontiers of war and violence alongside courageous co-workers. You risk your lives daily in order to reach out, humbly yet persistently, for what sometimes seems impossible, namely the peace and reconciliation longed for by Jesus Christ. We give thanks for the love and support offered by your families and for the friends who sustain and support you on a daily basis.

Through you, we greet also the men and women of the Jesuit Refugee Service and all those who share our mission in those Provinces and Regions where conflicts are strongest and most intractable. Without their contribution our mission would be considerably poorer. Living the same dangers, threats, and violence, you are brought together by the ties of friendship, prayer, and solidarity.

Sometimes, in such a mission, you may feel forgotten, laboring in different parts of the globe, far from the spotlight of media. In this special message we call you to mind, pray for you and ask the whole Society to do the same. You remain at difficult frontiers, seeing, in those who suffer, the face of Jesus who remains a constant friend and companion.

We thank God for the witness of friendship and hope that you offer. We are grateful for the many blessings you receive from the people you serve, blessings that enrich the whole Society of Jesus. You are not alone, you are part of an apostolic body whose sole consolation is to be placed with the Son in his suffering as well as in his glory. Your "offering of great price"[1] contributes to the strength and efficacy of the Society all over the world.

We thank you, dear friends in the Lord, because through your consecration to the mission of Christ, you accept poverty with Christ poor, even at times humiliation with the humiliated Christ. You can rightfully make yours the words of Saint Paul:

> *Who will separate us from the love of Christ? Will hardship, or distress, or persecution, or famine, or nakedness, or peril, or sword? [...]. No, in all these things we are more than conquerors through him who loved us.* (Rom. 8:35, 37)

Your Jesuit training has given you many gifts, prepared you for difficult struggles and enabled you to draw profit from every situation. You can face hardships and dangers with confidence. However, we are aware that those same hardships and dangers can erode you spiritually and affectively. That is why, on these fragile frontiers where you stand, discernment is vital as well as mutual care and solidarity. And when you experience powerlessness before the endless stories of wounded dignity or that meaningless drive to destruction, may you remember Jesus Christ who went through the same powerlessness and set his hope in the Father. He will sustain you. He who has called you is faithful and is working to make all things new.

Brothers, because the Society of Jesus is a Society of love and a communion of minds and hearts,[2] your names are close to our hearts. We are one body of friends in the Lord. We want to receive your news, to listen to your hopes and frustrations, and to discern the right ways of solidarity with you. We want also our news to reach you, our successes and our failures to be known to you, so that you can rejoice with us, grieve with us, and pray with us.[3]

---

[1] *Spiritual Exercises,* 97.

[2] ". . . and also because it seems to me that 'Society of Jesus' means to say 'a Society of love and conformity of minds,' and not 'of severity and servile fear.'" Francis Xavier, Letter to Ignatius (12 January 1549), § 5 (*MHSI,* MX II, Letter 70).

[3] "Later, in Malacca, I was given many letters from Rome and Portugal, and I received, and am receiving, so much consolation from them whenever I read them, and I read them very frequently, that it seems to me that though I am here, my dearest brothers, I am there with you, and if not in body, at least in spirit." Francis Xavier, Letter to his companions in Europe (10 November 1545) § 2 (*MHSI,* MX I, Letter 52).

Like you, we sometimes feel helpless before the myriad causes of war and violence. They can seem, and indeed often are, totally beyond our control. Whatever the reason, as always, it is the poorest of the poor who suffer. With you, we cry out against such injustice, we protest the suffering of so many innocent people.

A Radical Witness across All Continents

We take this opportunity to acknowledge the testimony of humble service of all who have given their lives in such situations. The list[4] includes Frans van der Lugt, a Dutch Jesuit priest who, living in Syria, was killed in Homs during 2014; the Jesuits and their co-workers martyred in El Salvador in 1989; and, in the years in between, many others across all continents. Theirs is a testimony to the power of the Gospel; to the beautiful but painful fragility of human life; to a commitment to a ministry of friendship; to the need to witness, even to the point of death; to the fact that suffering, risk, and the call to courage are part of our Jesuit lives and of our Christian vocation.

We remember Paolo Dall'Oglio, the Italian Jesuit priest abducted in Syria in July 2013 whose whereabouts are still unknown. We pray to God that he can come back to us and to his family. We give God thanks for the safe release of Prem Kumar, the Indian Jesuit priest who was kidnapped in Afghanistan and held for over eight months.

Changing Minds and Hearts

It is only through the Spirit of God that attitudes that generate and sustain these conflicts can really be changed. And so, the Congregation asks Jesuits throughout the world to pray for a conversion of hearts and minds through individual prayer and in our celebration of the Eucharist, and to invite others to do the same. Secondly, we encourage all Provinces to advocate for peace using whatever means are available, be they networks, social centers, educational institutions, parishes or publications. Thirdly, we remember the words of Pope Paul VI: "If you want peace, work for justice."[5] They remind us that, as we work for justice across the globe, we take part in this struggle for peace.

A Mission at the Heart of Our Jesuit Vocation

This struggle for justice, peace, and reconciliation brings us back to our Jesuit roots in the *Formula of the Institute*. It has been reiterated in recent General Congregations and is as relevant—and as urgent—today as it was when our First Companions founded the Society of Jesus. This mission at the frontier of war

---

[4] A full list of those killed since 1973 can be found in *Promotio iustitiae* 117.

[5] Paul VI, "Message for the Celebration of the Day of Peace 1 January 1972," *AAS* 63 (1971): 868.

and peace is a mission that touches us all whether we are Jesuit novices, scholastics, brothers, priests, those in active ministry, or those who have retired and may be in Province infirmaries. It touches us whether we are working in a parish or a theology faculty, a school, a spirituality center or other ministry. It calls us to a deeper life in community as well as to personal healing and conversion since we know that, ultimately, the roots of conflict lie in the divisions within the human heart.

The Risen Lord Brings Hope, Healing, and Consolation

Our hearts may be divided, but "God is greater than our hearts."[6] The Spirit of God is active all across our world, this Spirit of the resurrected Jesus who can touch even situations that seem hopeless and can bring new life and healing where it is most needed. We know that our faith can overcome any darkness, that our hope can build bridges, and that our love can heal. But this is not to say there are easy answers. The Cross of Good Friday and the silent waiting of Holy Saturday are so often starkly with us. It is precisely there that the Risen Jesus comes to meet us as Consoler and Friend. Our desire is to extend his friendship to those affected and brutalized by conflict, even to those seen as enemies. We have no weapons except this friendship. It opposes the dynamics of violence, gathers us as Friends in the Lord, and calls us to love and serve in all things, together with so many other friends with whom we cooperate, we celebrate, we communicate. Faced with huge challenges and even apparent failure, we still dare to dream of creating with them a different world because we know the One whose "power working in us can do infinitely more than we can ask or imagine."[7] And so we stand firm, "wearing for shoes [...] the eagerness to spread the Gospel of peace."[8]

Hearts on Fire: Preaching the Good News Wherever the Need Is Greatest

Working at the frontiers, you are risking your lives. You represent something at the heart of our Jesuit vocation, the desire, lived so imaginatively and with such passion by Francis Xavier and the early companions, to go and preach the Good News whatever the risk and wherever the need is greatest.

As we write this message to you, we feel ourselves linked to the wellspring of our vocation. We find our hearts on fire, the fire our Lord came to bring to earth.[9] And so we are consoled. With you, we are moved with compassion, a compassion that translates into a strong desire to change the painful realities we see portrayed on our screens. With you, we want to bring about the

---

[6] 1 John 3:20.
[7] Eph. 3:20.
[8] Eph. 6:15.
[9] Luke 12:49.

reconciliation that Jesus Christ desires and that our world needs so badly. With you, we place ourselves at the foot of his Cross, asking how best we can serve and love, how best we can act for change, how best we can be channels of the Spirit of God into our broken world. With these deep and great desires, yet humbly knowing our limitations and aware of our smallness in this *minima Societas,* we make the following prayer:

> *Lord our God,*
>
> *We come before you to pray for our brothers who serve you at the frontiers of violence and war.*
>
> *We place under your protection our companions present in Syria and South Sudan, Colombia, and the Great Lakes region of Africa, the Central African Republic, Afghanistan, Ukraine, Iraq, and so many other places. Together with so many partners in their mission, they share the consequences of war and violence with millions of women, men, and children. Grant them your consolation. Be their strength.*
>
> *You who are the Father of Peace, bring your peace to our world. Let it grow in the hearts of world leaders. Let it spread to the people of all parts of the world and of all beliefs. Let your love lead our world.*
>
> *Finally, we recall those injured or killed while serving your mission in war zones. They show in their bodies the passion that animates the Society. May the living find comfort in the bread broken in the Eucharist, and the departed enjoy the light of your face in the Kingdom of your peace.*
>
> *We ask you this though our Lord Jesus Christ. Amen.*
>
> *Mary, Queen of Peace and Mother of the Society of Jesus, pray for us.*

Matters Entrusted to Father General

Interprovincial Houses in Rome

GC 36 recommends that Father General study the issue of the renewal of the organization and structures of governance of the DIR (*Domus Interprovinciales Romanae*), in dialogue with the Permanent Interprovincial Commission and the members of the DIR.

Protection and Safety of Minors

GC36 asks Father General to continue working with Major Superiors and Conferences to promote, within the communities and ministries of the Society, a consistent culture of protection and safety for minors, in keeping with the suggestions of the Congregation regarding formation, community life, ministries, and governance.

Revision of the *Formulae*

The General Congregation directs and authorizes Father General to undertake a revision of the *Formulae*, to approve that revision, and to communicate the revised *Formulae* to the Society, after consulting the Major Superiors and receiving the approval of the General Council by deliberative vote. This revision should be completed within one year from the end of GC 36.

Modification of *Constitutions* 701 and 704

1. General Congregation 36 modifies *Const.* 701 in the following manner:

    "When the election does not take place in that manner, the following procedure should be followed. First, each one should pray privately and, without speaking with anyone else [C], make his decision in the presence of his Creator and Lord on the basis of the information he has. He will write on a piece of paper the name of the person whom he chooses for superior general, and signs it with his name. One hour at most should be given for this. Thereupon all should assemble in their seats. The vicar, together with a secretary to be chosen for this purpose from among the professed and by another to assist [D], should arise and attest his wish to admit no one he should not, nor to exclude anyone. **He should give to all general absolution from all censures for purposes of the canonical election [E].**[10] After the grace [...]."

2. General Congregation 36 modifies *Const.* 704 in the following manner:

    "**E. He absolves from all censures except those incurred through defects regarding the election.**"[11]

Revision of *Complementary Norm* 362

General Congregation 36 modifies *Complementary Norm* 362 in the following manner:

362 §1 Although the superior general is elected for life and not for any determined time,[12] he may nonetheless in good conscience and by law resign

---

[10] **Abolished by GC 36** (since the censures, according to the 1983 *Code of Canon Law* and the 1990 *Code of Canons of the Eastern Churches*, no longer have any effect on the right of election).

[11] **Abolished by GC 36** (since the censures, according to the 1983 *Code of Canon Law* and the 1990 *Code of Canons of the Eastern Churches*, no longer have any effect on the right of election).

[12] Cf. P. IX c.1 [719].

from his office for a just and proportionate cause[13] that would render him permanently unequal to the labors of his post.[14]

§2 When the superior general, either of his own accord but after consultation with the assistants for provident care, or after he has been so advised by them, will have judged that it is proper to resign his office, he should ask these assistants, the other general councillors, and the major superiors of the whole Society to take a secret vote whether the causes are just and proportionate. These votes should be counted in the presence of the assistants for provident care and the secretary of the Society. If a majority judges that a general congregation ought to be convoked for the purpose of making provision for the supreme government of the Society, the superior general ought to summon it.[15]

§3 But if a majority does not so judge, it is left entirely to the Superior General to do what in conscience seems best to him according to our Institute.

§4 When a general congregation is in session for other business, the superior general may propose his resignation to it for a just and proportionate cause[16] that would render him permanently unequal to the labors of his post, after consultation with the assistants for provident care.

§5 The Superior General's resignation from office does not take effect until it has been accepted by the Society in a General Congregation.[17]

Revision of *Complementary Norm* 396

Nº 396 of *Complementary Norms* is revised as follows:

Approximately every six years beginning from the last General Congregation the Superior General shall convoke a meeting of all Major Superiors, in order to consider the state, the problems, and the initiatives of the universal Society, as well as international and supra-provincial cooperation.

---

[13] Cf. CIC 187–189; Cf. CCEO, 967–971.
[14] Coll. D. 260 § 1 (GC 31, d. 41 n. 2 §1).
[15] Coll. D. 260 § 4 (GC 31, d. 41 n. 2 §4).
[16] Cf. CIC 187–189 § 2; Cf. CCEO, 967–971.
[17] Coll. D. 260 § 5 (GC 31, d. 41 n. 2 §5).

COMPLEMENTARY DOCUMENTATION

Address of His Holiness Pope Francis to the
36th General Congregation of the Society of Jesus

General Curia of the Society of Jesus
Monday, 24 October 2016

Editor's note: The following is a transcript of the address as given by the Holy Father. Comments that were not in the prepared text but added extemporaneously in the Aula are shown in italics and set between brackets.

My dear Brothers and Friends in the Lord, [*Good morning,*]

While I was praying about what to say to you today, a fond memory came to me of the last words Blessed Paul VI said to us at the opening of our 32nd General Congregation: "Così, così, fratelli e figli. Avanti, *in Nomine Domini. Camminiamo insieme*, liberi, obbedienti, uniti nell'amore di Cristo, per la maggior gloria di Dio.[1]

Saint John Paul II and Pope Benedict XVI also encouraged us *"to walk in a manner* worthy of the vocation to which we are called"[2] (cf. Eph 4:1) and "in the ecclesial and social context that marks the beginning of this millennium, [...] *to continue on the path* of this mission in full fidelity to your original charism. As my Predecessors have said to you on various occasions, the Church needs you, relies on you and continues to turn to you with trust, particularly to reach those physical and spiritual places which others do not reach or have difficulty in reaching.[3] To walk together—free and obedient—moving toward the margins of society where no one else reaches, "under the gaze of Jesus and looking to the horizon which is the ever greater glory of God, who ceaselessly surprises us.[4] As

---

[1] Paul VI, *Address to the 32nd General Congregation of the Society of Jesus*, 3 December 1974. ["This is the way, this is the way, brothers and sons. Forward, *in Nomine Domini!* Let us walk together, free, obedient, united in the love of Christ, for the greater glory of God" (Editor's note)].

[2] John Paul II, *Homily: Mass at the Opening of the 33rd General Congregation of the Society of Jesus*, 2 September 1983.

[3] Benedict XVI, *Address to the Participants of the 35th General Congregation of the Society of Jesus*, 21 February 2008.

[4] Francis, *Homily: Liturgical Memorial of the Most Holy Name of Jesus*, Church of the Gesù, 3 January 2014.

Saint Ignatius reminds us, a Jesuit is called "to think and to live in any part of the world where there is hope for greater service of God and help of souls" [*Constitutions*, 304]. The fact is that "for the Society, the world must be our house," as Nadal used to say.[5]

Saint Ignatius wrote to Francis Borgia about the criticism made by the Jesuits who were called "angelic" (Oviedo and Onfroy), [*a beautiful story*,] because they were saying that the Society was insufficiently founded and needed more grounding in the spirit: "the spirit that guides them," Ignatius wrote, "ignores the state of things in the Society which are always *in fieri*, except for what is absolutely necessary."[6] I rather like Ignatius's way of seeing everything—except for what is absolutely essential—as constantly developing (*in fieri*), because it frees the Society from all kinds of paralysis and wishful thinking.

What is necessary and essential is the *Formula of the Institute*, which we should keep constantly before our eyes after looking to God our Lord: "the nature of this Institute which is a pathway to God." This is the way it was for the First Companions, just as they foresaw it would be "for those who will follow us along this path." In this way, whether it be poverty or obedience or the dispensation from certain obligations such as praying in choir: all these things are neither demands nor privileges, but rather aids to the mobility of the Society, so that its members may be available "to run in the path of Christ Our Lord" (*Constitutions*, 582), having, thanks to their vow of obedience to the Pope, "more certain direction from the Holy Spirit" (*Formula of the Institute 1550, 3*). The *Formula* contains Ignatius's insight, and its essence is what accounts for the Constitutions' insistence on always keeping in mind the priority of "places, times, and persons," and the fact that all the rules are intended—*tantum quantum*—to help us in concrete situations.

For Ignatius the journey is not an aimless wandering; rather, it translates into something qualitative: it is a "gain" or progress, a moving forward, a doing something for others. This is how it is expressed in the two *formulas* of the Institute approved by Popes Paul III (1540) and Julius III (1550), centering on the Society's solicitude for the faith—its defense and propagation—and on the lives and instruction of the people. Here Ignatius and the First Companions use the word "aprovechamiento" or "benefit" (*ad profectum*,[7] cf. Phil 1:12, 25)

---

[5] *Monumenta Nadal* (MHSI), 5:364–365.

[6] *Letter 51, to Francis Borgia*, July 1549, 17, n. 9. Cf. Miguel Ángel Fiorito and Andrés Swinnen, "La Fórmula del Instituto de la Compañía de Jesús (introducción y versión castellana)," *Stromata* 3/4 (July–December 1977): 259–260.

[7] "Ad profectum animarum in vita et doctrina christiana," in *Monumenta Ignatiana: Constitutiones et regulae Societatis Iesu*, 4 vols. (Rome: MHSI, 1934), 26 and 376; cf. *Constituzioni della Compagnia di Gesù annotate dalla GC 34 e Norme complementari* (Rome: ADP, 1995), 32–33.

to describe the practical criterion of discernment in Ignatian spirituality, [*lo que más aprovecha, what is more helpful*].

Aprovechamiento, drawing profit or bearing fruit, is not individualistic but communal. "The end of this Society is to devote itself with God's grace not only to the salvation and perfection of the members' own souls, but also with that same grace to labor strenuously in giving aid toward the salvation and perfection of the souls of their neighbors" (*General Examen,* n. 3). And if Ignatius's heart was inclined in one direction or the other, it was toward helping the neighbors; so much so that he would get angry whenever he was told that someone wanted to join the Society "in order to save his soul. Ignatius did not want people who were good for their own sake if they were not apt for the service of their neighbors" (Aicardo I, point 10, p. 41).

Aprovechamiento pervades everything. Ignatius's *Formula* expresses an inherent tension: "not only . . . but . . .; this mentality of holding tensions together—one's own salvation and perfection with the salvation and perfection of others—beginning with the higher order of grace, is a distinctive characteristic of the Society. [*This pattern is always repeated, the mentality of uniting tensions.*] The harmonizing of this and all tensions (contemplation and action, faith and justice, charisma and institutions, community and mission . . .) is not contained in abstract formulas but rather obtained over the course of time through that which Favre calls "our way of proceeding."[8] By walking and "moving forward" in following the Lord, the Society harmonizes the tensions inevitably produced by the diversity of the people it brings together and the missions it receives.

Aprovechamiento is not elitist. In the *Formula,* Ignatius describes the means to more universal fruit that are specifically priestly. But first let us note that works of mercy are taken for granted in the *Formula.* It says: "without these being an obstacle" to mercy! The works of mercy—the care of the sick in the hospital, alms and their distribution, the teaching of the young, bearing hardships patiently—these were the milieus of life in which Ignatius and his First Companions moved and existed. These were their daily bread. They took great pains to prevent anything from getting in the way of these!

In the end, this kind of *aprovechamiento* is "whatever bears more fruit." It is a *magis,* that *plus* that leads Ignatius to undertake initiatives, to follow them through, and to evaluate their real impact on peoples' lives in matters of faith, justice, mercy, and charity. [*Initiating processes is different from occupying spaces. The Society initiates processes and leaves spaces. This is important. Other religious occupy spaces, the monasteries. The Society initiates processes.*] The *magis* is the fire, the fervor of action that rouses us from slumber. Our saints have always been an

---

[8] Cf. *Fabri Monumenta* (Rome: Institutum Historicum Societatis Iesu, 1972), 50, 69, 111, 114, etc.

incarnation of this. It was said of Saint Albert Hurtado that he was "a sharp dart stuck in the sleeping flesh of the Church."

This counters the temptation that Paul VI labeled *spiritus vertiginis* and what de Lubac called "spiritual worldliness." A temptation that is not primarily moral but spiritual as it distracts us from what is essential: namely, to be useful, to leave an imprint or a mark in history, especially in the lives of the smallest. "The Society is fervor," Nadal affirmed.[9] In order to reignite fervor in the mission of "benefiting" people in their concrete lives and through teaching, I would like to ground my reflections in three points which, given that the Society is in the places of mission in which it should be, especially enhance our way of proceeding. These three points are joy, the Cross, and the Church—our Mother—and they have the purpose of taking a step forward, taking away the impediments that the enemy of human nature places in front of us when, in the service of God, we rise from good to better.

1. Ask [Intensely] for Consolation

We can always improve in praying persistently for consolation. The two apostolic exhortations, along with *Laudato si'*, were meant to highlight the importance of joy. In the *Exercises,* Ignatius asks his companions to contemplate "the task of consolation" as something specific to the Resurrected Christ (*Spiritual Exercises,* 224). It is the specific task of the Society to console the Christian faithful and to help them in their discernment so that the enemy of human nature does not distract us from joy: the joy of evangelizing, the joy of the family, the joy of the Church, the joy of creation [...]. Let us never be robbed of that joy, neither through discouragement when faced with the great measure of evil in the world and misunderstandings among those who intend to do good, nor by letting it be replaced with vain joys that are easily bought and sold in any shop.

This "service of joy and spiritual consolation" is rooted in prayer. It consists in encouraging ourselves and others "to ask insistently for God's consolation." Ignatius expresses this in a negative formulation in the sixth rule of the first week when he affirms: "It is very helpful to intensify our activity against the same desolation" by persisting in prayer (*Spiritual Exercises,* 319). It is helpful because in desolation we realize how weak we are without grace and consolation (cf. *Spiritual Exercises,* 324). To practice and teach this prayer of asking and begging for consolation is our main service of joy. If one does not consider himself worthy (something that happens often in practice), he should at least persist in asking for this consolation out of a love for the message, since joy is constitutive of the Gospel, and he should ask it also out of a love for others, his family, and the world. One cannot deliver good news with a sullen face. Joy is

---

[9] Cf. *Monumenta Nadal* (Rome: Monumenta Historica Soc. Iesu, 1962), 5:310.

not a decorative "add-on" but a clear indicator of grace: it indicates that love is active, operative, present. Therefore searching for it should not be confused with searching for some "special effect" easily produced today for the mere purpose of consumption, but rather it should be sought in its essential trait of "permanence": Ignatius opens his eyes and awakes to this discernment of spirits by discovering the difference between the joys that endure and the joys that pass away (*Autobiography*, 8). Time becomes the element that offers him the key to recognizing the action of the Spirit. [*One of the expressions of deep joy is a sense of humor. I think it is a grace we have from God. To my way of thinking, the human attitude closest to divine grace is the sense of humor.*]

In the *Exercises,* progress in the spiritual life is made through consolation: it is "a moving from good to better" (cf. *Spiritual Exercises*, 315) as well as "every increase of hope, faith, and charity and all interior joy" (*Spiritual Exercises*, 316). This service of joy was what led Ignatius's First Companions to establish rather than disband the Society to which they offered themselves and shared spontaneously, and whose distinctive characteristic was the joy it gave them in praying together, being sent as missionaries together, and reuniting in imitation of the life that the Lord and His Apostles led. This joy of an explicit proclamation of the Gospel—by means of the preaching of the faith and the practice of justice and mercy—is what drives the Society out to the margins of society. The Jesuit is a servant of the joy of the Gospel, be it when he is working "in the workshop" of giving retreats—even if to one person, helping him or her to encounter that "interior place whence comes the strength of the Spirit that guides, frees, and renews"[10]—or when he is working in a structural way by organizing works of formation, mercy, and reflection, all of which are an institutional outgrowth of that point of "inflection" in which we allow our will to be overcome and the Holy Spirit comes into action. M[*ichel de*] Certeau said it well: the *Exercises* are "the apostolic method *par excellence*" insofar as they make possible "a return to the heart, to the principle of docility to the Spirit, who awakens and encourages whoever undertakes the exercises to personal fidelity to God."[11]

2. Allow Ourselves to Be Moved by the Lord on the Cross

We can always improve somewhat in allowing ourselves to be moved by the Lord on the cross, both in his person and as present in the sufferings of so many of our brothers and sisters—indeed, the majority of the human race! Just as Fr. Arrupe said, wherever there is pain, the Society is there [*or better said: has to be there*].

---

[10] Pierre Favre, *Mémorial* (Paris: Desclée, 1959); cf. "Introduction" by Michel de Certeau, 74.

[11] Ibid., 76.

The Jubilee of Mercy is a privileged time to reflect on the "services" of mercy. I use the plural because mercy is not an abstraction but a lifestyle consisting in concrete gestures rather than mere words: reaching out and touching the flesh of the neighbor and institutionalizing the works of mercy. For those of us who make the Exercises, this grace by means of which Jesus commands us to become like the Father (cf. Lk 6:36) begins with a colloquy of mercy that is an extension of our colloquy with the Lord crucified because of my sins. The entire second Exercise is a conversation full of sentiments of shame, confusion, sorrow, and tears of gratitude, seeing precisely who I am—by making myself small—and who God is—by magnifying him—he who "preserved my life until now"); and by seeing who Jesus is, hanging on the cross for me (*Spiritual Exercises*, 61 and previous numbers). The way in which Ignatius lives and formulates his experience of mercy is of great personal and apostolic benefit and requires a sharp and sustained experience of discernment. Our spiritual father said to Saint Francis Borgia: "As for me, I persuade myself both before and after that I am nothing but an obstacle; and from this I derive great spiritual contentment and joy in our Lord insofar as I cannot take credit for anything that appears good."[12] Ignatius therefore lives completely on God's mercy even in the littlest things. He felt that the greater the obstacle he raised, the greater the goodness with which the Lord treated him: "tanta era la misericordia del Signore, e tanta la copia della soavità e dolcezza della grazia sua con esso lui, che quanto egli più desiderava d'essere in questo modo castigato, tanto più benigno era Iddio e con abbondanza maggiore spargeva sopra di lui i tesori della sua infinita liberalità. Laonde diceva, che egli credeva non vi essere nel mondo uomo, in cui queste due cose insieme, tanto come in lui, concorressero; la prima mancare tanto a Dio, e l'altra il ricevere tante e così continue grazie dalla sua mano."[13] [*I quoted this in Italian because I did not find the Spanish text.*]

Ignatius, in formulating his experience of mercy in these comparative terms—the more he felt he was failing the Lord, the more the Lord showered him with His grace—liberated the dynamic strength of mercy that we so often dilute with abstract *formulae* and legalistic conditions. The Lord, who looks upon us with mercy and chooses us, sends us forth with the same powerful mercy to the poor, the sinners, the abandoned, the crucified, and anyone who

---

[12] Ignatius of Loyola, *Letter 26 to Francis Borgia*, c. 1545.

[13] Pedro de Ribadeneyra, *The Life of Saint Ignatius of Loyola* (Rome: La Civiltà Cattolica, 1863), 336. ["(...) the Lord's mercy was so great and the tenderness and sweetness of His grace so abundant within him, that the more he wished to be castigated in this way, the greater was God's goodness toward him and the more generously He showered him with the treasures of His infinite generosity. And so he said he believed there was no other man in the world in whom these two things came together more strikingly: failing God so much on the one hand, and receiving so many graces from Him on the other." (Editor's note)])

suffers from injustice and violence in today's world. Only when we experience this healing force in our own lives and in our own wounds [*wounds with first and last names*]—as individuals and as a body—will we be able to lose our fear of allowing ourselves to be moved by the immense suffering of our brothers and sisters so as to go out and walk patiently with our peoples, learning from them the best way to help and serve them (cf. *General Congregation*, 32, D. 4, n. 50).

3. Do Good with a Good Spirit by "Thinking with the Church"

We can also take a step forward in doing good with a good spirit: "thinking with the Church," as Saint Ignatius says. It is also a distinctive service of the Society to facilitate the discernment of *how* we do things. Favre formulated it by asking for the grace that "all the good that can be realized, thought, and organized, be done with a good spirit, not a bad spirit."[14] This grace of discerning, which is not limited to thinking, doing, and organizing the good, but also doing these things with a good spirit, is what roots us in the Church in which the Spirit works and distributes his various gifts for the common good. Favre used to say that in many cases those who wanted to reform the Church were right, but God did not wish to correct the Church using their methods, [*the methods they proposed*].

It is distinctive of the Society to do things by "thinking with the Church." To do this peacefully and joyfully, given the sins we perceive within ourselves and in the structures we have created, entails carrying the cross and experiencing poverty and humiliation, the locus in which Ignatius encourages us to choose between patiently enduring them and desiring them.[15] Whenever the contradiction was more pronounced, Ignatius set an example of reflecting before speaking or acting in order to work in a good spirit. The rules of "thinking with the Church" are not to be read as precise instructions on controversial points (some might be anachronistic), but rather as examples where Ignatius extended the invitation to "act against" the anti-ecclesial spirit of his time, inclining always and decisively on the side of our Mother, the Church; not to justify a controversial point, but rather to open up space in which the Spirit could work in his time.

The service of good-spiritedness and discernment makes us men of the Church—ecclesial men, not clerical men—men "for others," having nothing of our own that isolates us but placing everything we have in common and at the service of others.

We walk neither by ourselves nor for our own comfort; we walk with "a heart that does not rest, that does not close in on itself but beats to the rhythm

---

[14] Favre, *Mémorial*, n. 51.

[15] Cf. *Directorio autógrafo*, in *Exeritia spiritualia Sancti Ignatii de Loyola et eorum directoria*, 2 vols. (Rome: MHSI, 1955), 2:78 (n. 23).

of a journey undertaken together with all the faithful people of God."[16] We walk making ourselves all things to all people in order to help some.

This shedding of ourselves makes it possible for the Society to always have the face, the way of speaking, and the way of being of all peoples, all cultures, by inserting ourselves into all of them, into the specific heart of each people, to build up the Church with each of them, by inculturating the Gospel and evangelizing every culture.

Let us ask Our Lady of the Way, in a colloquy like that of a son with his mother or a servant with his Mistress, to intercede for us in the presence of the "Father of mercies and God of all consolation" (2 Cor. 1:3), that he may place us once again with his Son, with Jesus, who takes up the cross of the world and asks us to take it up with him. Let us entrust her with our "way of proceeding," that it may be ecclesial, inculturated, poor, ministerial, and free of worldly ambition. Let us ask our Mother to guide and accompany each Jesuit together with that portion of the faithful People of God to which he is sent, *on the ways of consolation, compassion, and discernment.*

---

[16] Francis, Homily: Liturgical Memorial of the Most Holy Name of Jesus, Church of the Gesù, 3 January 2014.

"To Have Courage and Prophetic Audacity"

Dialogue of Pope Francis with the Jesuits Gathered in the 36th General Congregation

On October 24, 2016, Pope Francis met the Jesuits gathered in their 36th General Congregation. A few minutes before 9:00 in the morning, he arrived in an ordinary car. After greeting Father General and the others who were waiting for him, he went to the Aula of the Congregation where he joined the delegates in prayer. Then he gave a speech. After a break, he entered into a time of frank and cordial dialogue with the delegates, who spontaneously asked him some questions. The pope did not want the questions to be selected beforehand, nor did he want to see them first. This gave life to a familial encounter that lasted about an hour and a half. At the end, Francis greeted those present one by one. We reproduce the questions and answers below. In the Aula, for practical reasons, the questions were asked in groups of three. The following text reproduces the pontiff's answers in their entirety and, for ease of reading, separates the questions, giving the basic thrust of each one. The text preserves the tone and meaning of the oral conversation.

Holy Father, you are a living example of prophetic audacity. How do you communicate that audacity so effectively? How can we do it, too?

Courage is not just about making noise, but about knowing how to do it well, when and how to do it. First of all one must discern whether one should make noise or not. Courage is constitutive of all apostolic action. And today, more than ever, we need courage and prophetic audacity. We need a *parresía*[17] for today, the prophetic audacity of having no fear. It is noteworthy that this was the first thing that John Paul II said when he was elected pope: "Do not be afraid." He knew all the problems of the Eastern countries and audacity led him to confront them all.

What is the prophetic audacity that is asked of us today? We must discern this. That is, where should this prophetic audacity be channeled? It is an attitude born of the *magis*.[18] And the *magis* is *parresía*. The *magis* is founded on

---

[17] Parresía is a Greek word prevalent in the Greek text of the New Testament. It indicates the courage and sincerity of the testimony. It is a word widely used in Christian tradition, especially at the beginning, sometimes as opposed to hypocrisy.

[18] The *magis* (more) in the Ignatian tradition comes from the famous maxim "ad maiorem Dei gloriam" (to the greater glory of God) and synthesizes a strong spiritual impulse. The work of the Jesuit is characterized by this *magis*, a living tension that reminds us how it is always possible to take a step forward from where we are, because our walk is in line with an ever more explicit manifestation of the glory of God. With the discernment of spirits we learn to recognize the good that dwells in each situation and to choose what leads to the greater good.

God who is always greater. Looking at that ever greater God, discernment deepens and seeks the places to channel the audacity. I believe that this is your work in this congregation: to discern "where" the *magis*, the prophetic audacity, the *parresía*, must be directed.

Sometimes, prophetic audacity joins with diplomacy, with a work of persuasion accompanied by strong signs. For example, prophetic audacity is called upon to combat widespread corruption in some countries. Corruption, to give an example, such as when the constitutional period of a term of office ends and one seeks to reform the constitution to remain in power. I believe that here the Society, in its work of teaching and raising social awareness, must work with audacity to convince everyone that a country cannot grow if it does not respect the legal principles which that country itself has put in place to ensure future governability.

Father, the way in which colonizers treated indigenous peoples has been a serious problem. The appropriation of the land by the colonizers was a grave event whose repercussions are felt today. What do you think about this?

In the first place, it must be said that today we are more aware of the significance of the richness of the indigenous peoples, especially when, both politically and culturally, other forces tend to suppress them even more through globalization conceived as a "sphere," a globalization where everything becomes standardized. Today, our prophetic audacity, our consciousness, must be on the side of inculturation. And our image of globalization should not be the sphere, but the polyhedron. I like the geometric figure of the polyhedron, because it is one but has different faces. It expresses how unity is created while preserving the identities of the peoples, of the persons, of the cultures. That is the richness that today we have to give to the process of globalization, because otherwise it is homogenizing and destructive.

The process of a standardizing and destructive globalization destroys the indigenous cultures that in fact should be recovered. And we must recover them with the correct hermeneutic, which facilitates this task. This hermeneutic is not the same as at the time of colonization. The hermeneutic of that time was to seek the conversion of the peoples, to widen the Church [...] thus abolishing the indigenous independence. It was a centralist type of hermeneutic, where the dominant empire somehow imposed its faith and culture. It is understandable that people thought this way at the time, but today a radically different hermeneutic is necessary. We have to interpret things differently, valuing each people, their culture, their language. We have to help this process of inculturation, which has become increasingly important since Vatican II.

I want to refer to attempts at inculturation that were present in the early days of the missions. These initiatives were born of an experience like that of

Paul with the Gentiles. The Holy Spirit very clearly showed him that the Gospel was to be inculturated in the Gentile peoples. The same thing was repeated in the era of missionary expansion. Consider, for example, the experience of Matteo Ricci and Roberto de' Nobili.[19] They were pioneers, but a hegemonic conception of Roman centralism stopped that experience, interrupted it. It prevented a dialogue in which cultures were respected. And this happened because they interpreted social customs with a religious hermeneutic. Respect for the dead, for example, was confused with idolatry. Here, hermeneutics play a central role. At this moment I believe that it is important, with this greater awareness that we have regarding indigenous peoples, to support the expression, the culture, of each one of them [...] and in the same way, evangelization, which also touches the liturgy and reaches the expressions of worship. And the Congregation for Divine Worship accepts this.

I end with a memory that touches on moral theology. When I was a student of theology, I was assigned to be a librarian. In reviewing a Mexican text on morality from the 1700s, written in a question-and-answer format, I found a question that said: "Is sexual union between a Spaniard and an indigenous woman a mortal sin?" The answer of the moralist, who was a Dominican, made me laugh: "The matter is serious, therefore it is a serious sin according to matter, but since the consequence of this would be one more Christian to enlarge the kingdom of God, it is not as serious as if it were in Europe."

In your speech you clearly proposed a morality that is based on discernment. How do you suggest that we proceed in the field of morality with regard to this dynamic of discernment of moral situations? It seems to me that it is not possible to stay with an interpretation of a subsumed application of the norm which is limited to seeing particular situations as cases of the general norm.

Discernment is the key element: the capacity for discernment. I note the absence of discernment in the formation of priests. We run the risk of getting used to "white or black," to that which is legal. We are rather closed, in general, to discernment. One thing is clear: today, in a certain number of seminaries, a rigidity that is far from a discernment of situations has been introduced. And that is dangerous, because it can lead us to a conception of morality that has a casuistic sense. It appears in different formulations, but it is always along the same line. I am very afraid of this. This is what I said in a meeting with the Jesuits in Kraków during the World Youth Day. There, the Jesuits asked me what I thought the

---

[19] The Jesuits Matteo Ricci (1552–1610) and Roberto de' Nobili (1577–1656) were true pioneers. Missionaries in China and India, respectively, they sought to adapt the proclamation of the Gospel to local culture and worship. But this caused some concern and, in the Church, voices were raised against the spirit of these behaviors, as if they were a contamination of the Christian message.

Society could do and I replied that an important task of the Society is to form seminarians and priests in discernment.

I and those of my generation, perhaps not the youngest here, but my generation and some of the later ones too, were educated in a decadent Scholasticism. We studied theology and philosophy with manuals. It was a decadent Scholasticism. For example, to explain the "metaphysical continuum"—it makes me laugh every time I remember—we were taught the theory of the "puncta inflatae."[20] When the great Scholasticism began to lose force, there arose that decadent Scholasticism with which at least my generation and others have studied.

It was this decadent Scholasticism that provoked the casuistic attitude. It is curious: the course on the "sacrament of penance," in the faculty of theology, in general—not everywhere—was presented by teachers of sacramental morality. The whole moral sphere was restricted to "you can," "you cannot," "up to here yes but not there." In an *ad audiendas* examination, a companion of mine, when asked a very intricate question, said very simply: "But Father, please, these things do not happen in reality!" And the examiner replied, "But it's in the books!"

It was a morality very foreign to discernment. At that time there was the "cuco,"[21] the specter of situational morality [...]. I think Bernard Häring[22] was the first to start looking for a new way to help moral theology to flourish again. Obviously, in our day moral theology has made much progress in its reflections and in its maturity; it is no longer a "casuistry."

In the field of morality we must advance without falling into situationalism: but, rather, it is necessary to bring forward again the great wealth contained in the dimension of discernment; this is characteristic of the great Scholasticism. We should note something: St. Thomas and St. Bonaventure affirm that the general principle holds for all but—they say it explicitly—as one moves to the particular, the question becomes diversified and many nuances arise without changing the principle. This Scholastic method has its validity. It is the moral method used by the *Catechism of the Catholic Church*. And it is the method that was used in the last apostolic exhortation, *Amoris laetitia*, after the discernment made by the whole Church through the two synods. The morality used in *Amoris laetitia* is Thomistic, but that of the great St. Thomas himself, not of the author of the "puncta inflatae."

---

[20] The pope refers to the theories debates of the beginning of the 1600s in which Jesuits like Rodrigo de Arriaga were involved.

[21] "Cuco" could be translated as "bogeyman."

[22] Bernard Häring (1922–98), a Redemptorist, was a German moral theologian and one of the founders of the "Academia Alfonsiana." His work had a significant influence on the preparation and development of the Second Vatican Council.

It is evident that, in the field of morality, one must proceed with scientific rigor, and with love for the Church and discernment. There are certain points of morality on which only in prayer can one have sufficient light to continue reflecting theologically. And on this, allow me to repeat it, one must do "theology on one's knees." You cannot do theology without prayer. This is a key point and it must be done this way.

About the Society there are many legends: positive ones, from those who like us, and stories that are a bit dark from those who do not. To you, who love us and know us well, I want to ask: what things would you like us to pay attention to?

For me it is a bit difficult to respond, because it is necessary to see where the criticisms come from. It is difficult because, in my situation and in the environment in which I move, criticisms of the Society have a predominantly restorationist flavor. In other words, they are criticisms that dream of a restoration of a Society that perhaps was once attractive, because that was its time, but that is no longer desirable in our day, because God's time for the Society today is no longer that. I think this is the kind of argumentation behind the criticism. But the Society on this point has to be faithful to what the Spirit tells it.

Critiques also depend on who makes them. We should discern where they come from. I think that sometimes even the most malicious critic can say something that helps me. I think we have to listen to all the critiques and discern them, and not close the door to any criticism, because we risk getting used to closing doors. And that's not good. After discernment one can say: this criticism has no foundation and I can set it aside. But we must submit to discernment all of the criticism that we hear, I would say daily, personally, but always with good will, with openness of heart and before the Lord.

We live in a world characterized by political and religious polarizations. You, in fact, have lived different experiences in your life, as provincial and as archbishop of Buenos Aires. From your experience, what suggestions for us can you make of ways to confront these situations of polarization, especially when our brothers are involved in them?

I think that politics in general, big politics, has been increasingly degraded into small politics. Not only in partisan politics within each country, but also in sectoral politics within the same continent. I wanted to address this specific question—because I was asked—with the three speeches about Europe, the two in Strasburg and the one of the "Charlemagne" Prize. The French bishops have just issued a communique on politics that takes up again or follows upon one from fifteen or twenty years ago, "Réhabiliter la politique," which was very important. That declaration was timely: it gave force to politics, to politics as craftsmanship used to build the unity of peoples and the unity of a people with all the diversity that is within them. In general, the opinion I hear is that politicians are on the wane. Countries lack those great politicians who were able to spend themselves seriously for their ideals and were not afraid of dialogue or struggle, but went ahead, with intelligence and with the charism specific to politics. Politics is one of the highest forms of charity. Great politics. And in that I think that polarization does not help. On the contrary, what helps in politics is dialogue.

What is your experience with the brothers in the Society, in terms of their role, and how can one attract those with the vocation to be a brother in the Society?

My experience with the brothers has always been very positive. The brothers with whom I lived during my time as a student were wise men, very wise. They had a wisdom different from that of scholastics or that of the priests. Today, even brothers who have studied a great deal and who have leadership positions in the institutions still have an "I do not know what" that is different from the priests. And I think this has to be preserved, the wisdom, that special sapiential quality that comes from being a brother.

What's more, in the brothers I knew, I was impressed by their special sense, the ability to "smell" that they had when they said, for example: "Watch that father, I think he needs special help . . ." The brothers I have known often had great discretion. And they helped! The brother realized, before any other community members, what was happening. I do not know how to express it, I believe that there is a specific grace here and we must find what God's will is for the brother right now, and we also have to find how to express it.

I would like to hear you say when the prophecy of Isaiah will be fulfilled: "They will beat their swords into plowshares [...]" In my continent, Africa, we already have enough means to kill each of us ten times.

Working for peace is urgent. I said, more than a year and a half ago, that we are in World War III, in bits and pieces. Now the bits are gathering more and more. We are in war. Do not be naive. The world is at war and several countries pay the price. Let us think of the Middle East, of Africa: there is a situation of continuous war. Wars that derive from a whole history of colonization and exploitation. It is true that countries have their independence, but often the country that gave them independence has reserved the subsoil for itself. Africa remains a target of exploitation for the riches it has. Even from countries that previously did not even think about this continent. Africa is always viewed from the perspective of exploitation. And clearly this provokes wars.

In addition, in some countries there is the problem of ideologization, which causes major fractures. I believe that working for peace at this juncture, besides being one of the beatitudes, is a priority. When will peace come? I do not know if it will come before the coming of the Son of Man, but I do know, on the other hand, that we have to work for peace as much as possible, through politics, through coexistence. It can come. It can. With the Christian attitudes that the Lord shows us in the Gospel, much can be done, much is done, and we move forward. Sometimes this comes at a high price, in first person. And still we go ahead. Martyrdom is part of our vocation.

Can we be saved alone? What is the relationship between community salvation and personal salvation?

No one is saved alone. I believe that this principle must be kept very clear: salvation is for the People of God. No one is saved alone. The one who wishes to save himself, along his own path of fulfillment, will end with that adjective that Jesus uses so many times: hypocrite. He ends in hypocrisy. To be saved alone, to attempt to save oneself, with an elitist attitude, is hypocrisy. The Lord has come to save everyone.

Is it good to study theology in a real-life context?

My advice is that everything that young people study and experience in their contact with different contexts, be also subject to personal and community discernment and taken to prayer. There must be academic study, contact with real life not only at the periphery but at the boundary of the periphery, prayer and personal and community discernment. If a community of students does all this, I am at peace. When one of those things is missing, I start to worry. If study is lacking, then one can say nonsense or idealize situations in a simplistic way. If there is no real and objective context, accompanied by those who know the environment and help, foolish idealisms can arise. If there is a lack of prayer and discernment, we can be very good sociologists or political scientists, but we will not have the evangelical audacity and the evangelical cross that we must carry, as I said at the beginning.

The Society, after GC 35, has gone some way toward the understanding of environmental challenges. We received Laudato si' *with joy. We feel that the pope has opened doors for dialogue with institutions. What more can we continue to do in order to continue to feel involved in this issue?*

Laudato si' is an encyclical on which many have worked, and the scientists who worked on it were asked to say well founded things and not simple hypotheses. Many people worked on the encyclical. My work, in effect, was to set the guidelines, to make a few corrections and then to prepare the final edition, yes, with my style and elaborating some things. And I think we must continue to work, through movements, academically, and also politically. In fact, it is evident that the world is suffering, not only because of global warming but because of the misuse of things and because nature is mistreated.

One must also take into account, in the interpretation of *Laudato si'*, that it is not a "green encyclical." It is a social encyclical. It begins with the reality of this moment, which is ecological, but it is a social encyclical. It is evident that those who suffer the consequences are the poorest, those who are discarded. It is an encyclical that confronts this culture of discarding people. We have to work hard on the social part of the encyclical because the theologians who worked on it were very concerned to show how much social impact the ecological facts have. It helps a lot to look at this as a social encyclical.

Does Pope Francis want a poor Society for the poor? What advice do you give us for walking in that direction?

I think that on this point of poverty St. Ignatius has gone far beyond us. When one reads how he thought about poverty, and about that vow that requires us not change poverty unless to make it more strict, we have to reflect. The view of St. Ignatius is not just an ascetic attitude, as if to pinch me so that it pains me more, but it is a love of poverty as a way of life, as a way of salvation, an ecclesial way. Because for Ignatius, and these are two key words that he uses, poverty is both mother and bulwark. Poverty nurtures, mothers, generates spiritual life, a life of holiness, apostolic life. And it is a wall, it defends. How many ecclesial disasters began because of a lack of poverty, including outside the Society, I mean in the whole Church in general. How many of the scandals which I, unfortunately, have to find out about, are born of money. I believe that St. Ignatius had a very great intuition. In the Ignatian vision of poverty, we have a source of inspiration to help us.

Clericalism, which is one of the most serious illnesses that the Church has, distances itself from poverty. Clericalism is rich. If it is not rich in money, it is rich in pride. But it is rich: there is in clericalism an attachment to possession. It does not allow itself to be nurtured by mother poverty, it does not allow itself to be guarded by the wall of poverty. Clericalism is one of the forms of wealth that we suffer from most seriously in the Church today. At least in some places of the Church. Even in the most everyday experiences. The poor Church for the poor is the Church of the Gospel, the Sermon on the Mount of the Gospel of Matthew, and the Sermon on the Plain of the Gospel of Luke, as well as the "protocol" according to which we will be judged: Matthew 25. I believe that the Gospel is very clear about this and it is necessary to walk in this direction. But I would also insist that it would be good for the Society to help deepen Ignatius's vision of poverty, because I believe it is a vision for the whole Church. Something that can help us all.

You spoke very well of the importance of consolation. When you reflect at the end of each day, what things give you consolation, and what things take consolation away from you?

I am talking to family, so I can say it: I am rather pessimistic, always! I am not saying that I am depressive, because that is not true. But it is true that I tend to focus on what did not work well. So for me consolation is the best antidepressant I have ever found! I find it when I stand before the Lord, and let Him manifest what He has done during the day. When at the end of the day I realize that I have been led, when I realize that despite my resistance, there was a driving force there, like a wave that carried me along, this gives me consolation. It is like feeling, "He is here." With regard to my pontificate, it consoles me to feel interiorly: "It was not a convergence of votes that got me into this dance, but that He is in there." This consoles me. And when I notice the times when my resistances have won, that makes me feel sorrow and leads me to ask for forgiveness. This is quite common [...] and it does me good. To realize that, as St. Ignatius says, one is "all impediment," to recognize that one has his resistances and that every day he lives them and that sometimes he overcomes them and sometimes he does not. This experience keeps one in his place. This helps. This is my personal experience, in the simplest possible terms.

The exhortation Evangelii gaudium *is very inspiring and encourages us to talk more about the theme of evangelization. What do you mean by the last words, in which you exhort us to continue the debate?*

One of the dangers of the pope's writings is that they create a little enthusiasm, but then others come along and the preceding ones are filed away. That is why I think it is important to continue working, hence that final indication that meetings are to be held and the message of *Evangelii gaudium* is to be deepened: it expresses a way of facing different ecclesial problems and evangelization for the Christian life. I think that you were referring to an exhortation that is at the end, and that comes from the *Aparecida* document. In that passage, we wanted to refer to *Evangelii nuntiandi,* which continues to have the freshest timeliness, as it had when it first came out, and that for me remains the most important pastoral document written after Vatican II. However, it is not mentioned, it is not cited. Well, the same thing can happen with *Evangelii gaudium.* A few days ago, I read that it would be necessary to take up again the point about the homily in *Evangelii gaudium,* because it had passed into silence. There is something that the Church has to correct in her preaching and that takes away a clericalist element. I believe that *Evangelii gaudium* has to be deepened, it must be worked on by groups of the laity, of priests, in the seminaries, because it is the evangelizing breath that the Church wants to have today. In this we have to move forward. It is not something finished, as if we were to say, "that's over, now comes *Laudato si'.* And then, "that's over, too, now it is on to *Amoris laetitia.*" By no means! I recommend *Evangelii gaudium* to you as a framework. It is not original, in this I want to be very clear. It puts together *Evangelii nuntiandi* and the *Aparecida* document. Although it came after the synod on evangelization, *Evangelii gaudium's* strength was to return to those two documents, to refresh them, and to offer them again in a new presentation. *Evangelii gaudium* is the apostolic framework of the Church today.

The Church is experiencing a decline in vocations, especially in places where she has been reluctant to promote local vocations.

It happened to me in Buenos Aires, as bishop, that very good priests, more than once, chatting with me, said: "In the parish I have a layman 'who is worth gold!'" They would describe him as a first-class layman and then ask, "Do you think we can make him a deacon?" This is the problem: the layman who is valuable, we make him into a deacon. We clericalize him. In a letter I recently sent to Cardinal Ouellet, I wrote that in Latin America the only thing more or less saved from clericalism is popular piety. In fact, since popular piety is one of those things "of the people" that priests did not believe in, lay people were creative. It may have been necessary to correct some things, but popular piety was saved because the priests did not get involved in it. Clericalism does not allow growth, it does not allow the power of baptism to grow. The grace and evangelizing power of the missionary expression comes from the grace of baptism. And clericalism controls this grace badly and gives rise to dependencies, which sometimes have whole peoples in a state of very great immaturity. I remember the fights that took place when I was a student of theology or a young priest and the base ecclesial communities appeared. Why? Because the laypeople began to have strong leadership, and the first ones who felt insecure were some of the priests. I am generalizing too much, but I do this on purpose: if I caricature the problem it is because the problem of clericalism is very serious.

With regard to local vocations, I say that the vocational decline will be spoken of at the next synod. I believe that vocations exist, you just have to know how to propose them and how to attend to them. If the priest is always in a hurry, if he is involved in a thousand administrative things, if we do not convince ourselves that spiritual direction is not a clerical charism, but a lay charism (which the priest can also develop), and if we do not call upon the laity in vocational discernment, it is evident that we will not have vocations.

Young people need to be heard; and the young can be tiring. They always come with the same issues and you have to listen to them. And of course, for this you have to be patient, to be seated and to listen. And also to be creative: you have to put them to work on things. Today, always having "meetings" no longer makes much sense, they are not fruitful. Young people should be sent on activities that are missionary, catechetical, or social, and these do a lot of good.

Once I came to parish on the periphery, in a shantytown. The priest had told me that he was building a meeting room. And since this priest also taught at the state university, he had aroused enthusiasm and desire among both boys and girls to participate. I arrived on a Saturday and they were working as masons: the engineer who was running everything was Jewish, one of the girls was an atheist, and the other, I do not know what, but they were united in a common job. This experience led to the question: Can I do something for others and with others? You have to put young people to work and listen to them. I would say these two things.

Not promoting local vocations is suicide, it is directly sterilizing a Church, the Church who is mother. Not promoting vocations is an ecclesial tubal ligation. It does not allow that mother to have her children. And that is serious.

Digitalization is the typical feature of this modern age. It creates speed, tension, crises. What is its impact on today's society? What can be done to have both speed and depth?

The Dutch, thirty years or more ago, invented a word: "rapid-ize." That is, a geometric progression in terms of velocity; and it is this "rapid-izing" that turns the digital world into a potential threat. I do not speak here of its positive aspects because we all know them. I also emphasize the problem of liquidity, which can cancel out what is concrete. Someone told me a while ago of a European bishop who went to see a businessman friend. He showed the bishop how, in ten minutes, he was completing an operation that made some profit. From Los Angeles he sold cattle to Hong Kong and in a few minutes had a profit that was immediately credited to his account. The liquidity of the economy, the liquidity of labor: all this causes unemployment. And a liquid world. One wants to call for a "return," although I do not like the word because it is a bit nostalgic. "Volver" is the title of an Argentine tango! There is a desire to recover the concrete dimension of work. In Italy, 40% of young people aged 25 and under are unemployed; in Spain 50%; in Croatia 47%. It is an alarm signal that shows that this liquidity creates unemployment.

Thank you for the questions and the liveliness of the conversation, and forgive me if I have spoken too freely.

〜

At the end of the dialogue, Fr. Arturo Sosa, S.J., Superior General of the Society of Jesus, greeted the pope with these words:

Holy Father, at the end of these two sessions, on behalf of all the companions gathered in the 36th General Congregation, I want to thank you from my heart for your fraternal presence among us and, thanks be to God, for speaking freely! Thank you for your contribution to our discernment.

We are grateful that you have confirmed the invitation to live our charism deeply, walking with the Church and so many men and women of goodwill, moved by compassion, determined to console by reconciling, sensitive to discern the signs of the times.

To walk without giving in to the temptation to stay in one of the many beautiful corners we find along the way. To walk, moved by the freedom of the Children of God that makes us available to be sent anywhere, encountering a suffering humanity, following the dynamic of the incarnation of the Lord Jesus, relieving the suffering of so many brothers and sisters, placed, like Him, on the cross.

We will walk together, according to our way of proceeding, without dissolving the tensions between faith and justice, dialogue and reconciliation, contemplation and action. . . . A path that leads us to a deep encounter with the human richness expressed in cultural diversity. We will continue our efforts of inculturation in order to better announce the gospel and to show forth the intercultural face of our common Father.

We will faithfully follow your advice to join in your unceasing prayer to receive the consolation that will make of each Jesuit, and of all men and women who share the mission of Christ, servants of the joyful news of the Gospel.

With grateful hearts, we now would like to greet you personally.

Words of Gratitude to Fr. Adolfo Nicolás, S.J.

Dearest Father Adolfo,

I have been asked to offer you, on behalf of the Congregation and, in a certain sense, of the whole Society of Jesus, some words of thanks, as you conclude your service as superior general, following the acceptance of your resignation.

This was a mission that the Society entrusted to you more than eight years ago, on the 19th of January 2008, in this very Aula, when you were elected by very large majority. This election brought joy to all the participants in the 35th Congregation, who were fully confident that, entrusting into your hands the leadership of our Society, they had made the right choice.

Today, looking back on these years when you were our Father General, we thank the Lord for all the good that has come to us, to the Society of Jesus spread throughout the world, to the Church and to all the people to whom we offer our service.

Thank you for your personal style. All who have known and encountered you speak of your cordiality, spontaneity, and simplicity, of your accessibility, of your friendly relationship with all, whether with simple persons or with those of high rank. Those who have lived with you in the Curia for years have been struck by your always smiling expression and your good humor; they do not recall ever having seen you looking distant, grim, tense or least of all angry.

Your warm participation in the community gatherings you have attended has nurtured affection and trust, openness, and confidence on the part of the brothers from all parts of the world, who have felt encouraged in their apostolic work. You have been a superior regarded with fondness, perceived to be close and fraternal—in a word, loved.

Thanks for your ability to inspire our religious life and our commitment to the mission.

You have constantly reminded us of the universal character of our mission, beyond the narrow confines of regions, nations or provinces, and invited us to spiritual depth, to avoid the risk of mediocrity and superficiality. "Universality" and "depth" are two words that we often heard from you and that we will not forget. You urged us not to be "distracted" Jesuits, but to "feel and savor things interiorly" so as to go to the heart of the problems, of the apostolic challenges of our time, using intelligence, study, and the heart to see the world with the eyes of God. You wanted us to know how to share the joys and anxieties, the questions of our brothers and sisters, to accompany them in seeking and finding the signs of the presence and the will of God, the movements of the Spirit beneath the superficial veneer, the external image of this globalized and frenetic world, characterized by the new digital culture.

You have given us the example of a serene wisdom, expressed in homilies rich in images and profound points for reflection, in the invitation to integrity in our religious life, towards the reality of daily conversion. These homilies were drawn from your rich spiritual experience and from your apostolic life, in which we heard, not infrequently, the echo of mission toward the great horizons of Asia.

These gifts of your person and your way of being, however, do not diminish the fact that you have given yourself very much to the work of governance, in order to respond to the expectations that the Society expressed in the 35th General Congregation. In these years, under your guidance and your encouragement, the great work of restructuring of provinces in different parts of the world took place. Major superiors were often invited to be forward-looking and to discern about the perhaps excessive number of works and ministries in areas under their responsibility. The conferences of provincials and their presidents were encouraged in the task of responding to challenges that go beyond the provincial or regional boundaries.

The General Curia was a laboratory of very dynamic and creative experimentation in new ways of serving the universal Society. You did not have an individualistic and centralizing style of governance, but rather one that was open to receiving help, to involving your closest collaborators in shared and co-responsible work as a team. There was frequent and effective use of working groups and committees to address complex problems, as well as the establishment, reorganization and enhancement of secretariats, such as those for ecumenism and interreligious dialogue, for secondary and higher education.

The Archives and the Historical Institute were reorganized as well. Work environments were restructured and made more welcoming and functional. The buildings of the Curia and the Via dei Penitenzieri were completely renovated, and now finally, the Aula in which we find ourselves is a worthy culmination of all this work done by your governance team.

You reminded us that the intellectual apostolate must continue to be one of the characteristics of the Society's service to the Church and to the world, and you effectively encouraged the commitment of our whole Order in supporting the institutions and missions which the Holy See has entrusted to her in Rome for the good of the universal Church.

You have promoted among us that which could be called a "culture of responsibility." The English language is very fond of the word "accountability": to give an account, to respond to tasks and trust received. This applies to all our responsibilities, in the apostolate as well as in governance.

In particular, you have ensured that the Society would be enabled to deal with grave situations in which it has been and is necessary to intervene, for example with regard to the abuse of minors, in which we, along with the whole community of the Church, have had to take the painful path of responding to crimes committed, of conversion and purification. There remains more to do for us to become real advocates of safeguarding and protection of minors, but much has already been done.

There are also other important aspects of your leadership of the Society that we do not want to forget.

You have been very busy and have traveled much, first to get to know the universal Society, particularly those areas you had not known before being elected; and then to make yourself familiar and present, to encourage, to participate, to know more deeply. You wrote many letters, delivered many speeches, and engaged in many conversations, participated in countless colloquies with active and attentive listening. In the numerous provinces you visited—almost all—and in meetings in which you participated, you were always welcomed with joy and gratitude, as a source of inspiration and guidance, both by Jesuits, and by our collaborators and friends. You did not hold back in your service to the universal Society, but you gave of yourself generously and joyfully. You did not belong to yourself but to the Lord and His Society: concretely—in the last eight years—to us. For all this, we are grateful to you.

At the Congregation of Procurators, held for the first time in Africa, in Nairobi in 2012, you wanted, through your extensive report on the state of the Society, to offer us an objective and profound reading of the positive as well as negative aspects of our situation, so that we could make a proper examination of conscience. We have not forgotten your acute description of three types of Jesuits: those fully available for the mission; those who, although working well, are not as free as the Ignatian *magis* requires; and those who, unfortunately, have a "serious lack of freedom." That report is still a valuable document today and has helped us to prepare ourselves for this General Congregation which is now beginning its decisive phase.

We do not wish to forget the insight with which you took the occasion of the second centenary of the restoration of the Society, in 2014, to revive in us a sense of our extraordinary history and the responsibility that comes from it, as well as a common consciousness and self-understanding of our identity and mission.

But your encouraging and inspiring guidance has also been appreciated beyond the Society of Jesus. You were for some time vice-president, and then president of the Union of Superiors General. Religious, both men and women, have appreciated and benefited from your service. As the popes have reminded us several times, we cannot disregard the fact that the Society has always had a role and a responsibility for apostolic religious life in the Church. You have represented and personified this responsibility well. It is not by chance that the superiors general elected you to represent them during the synods of these years. There, your interventions were marked by freedom of spirit, originality, courage, and breadth of perspective, demonstrating the breadth of your experience, your familiarity with diverse cultures and conditions of life in the Church, the need for a renewal of the theology of mission. We have reason to believe that you also played a role in encouraging Pope Francis to renew the methodology of the synod. It is not surprising that, in the two synods dedicated to the family, you were called by him to take active part in the commission that undertook the formidable work of synthesis in drafting the final report.

The General guides us, but also represents us in our relations with the other bodies of the Church and her universal government. You have dedicated yourself personally, to ensuring good and constructive relations with the various dicasteries of the Roman Curia, visiting the highest officials regularly. And Jesuits have felt themselves in good hands when you took their problems upon yourself, knowing that you knew how to take up their cause with clarity and firmness, and to come to their defense when it was fair and necessary. They have felt guided with quiet confidence, in an attitude of service that was not servile, in the spirit of a genuine and adult *sentire cum Ecclesia*, in accordance with the desire of St. Ignatius and the characteristics of our Society.

Finally, you were the first general to find himself in the situation—for most of us truly unexpected and difficult to imagine—of witnessing the election of a Jesuit pope; a Jesuit who, before being bishop and cardinal had been provincial, who had participated in two general congregations in this Aula, and whom we now see looking out from the Loggia of St. Peter's clothed in white. A historically unprecedented circumstance, the implications of which we will have the opportunity to consider in the course of this congregation. But now we thank you.

We thank you very much because from the start, you, for your part, were able to establish with Pope Francis a relationship of direct and friendly communication, the benefits of which the whole Society immediately experienced. You did so with that characteristic simplicity and discretion of yours, that has spared the Society and all of us any difficulty in the novelty of the situation. The Society of Jesus has continued, as always, to put itself completely at the disposal of the pope for the missions, and at the same time, the Society has felt with the pope, on many occasions, that spiritual harmony that flows naturally from our shared identity and religious spirituality, and which has in turn further enkindled in us the love and the desire to serve the Vicar of Christ in his service of the Church and of humanity: Living the mission in the Church and with a Church "moving outwards," called to proclaim Jesus and to serve on the frontiers and in the peripheries, feeling ourselves walking with the people of God, in solidarity with the poor and all who suffer, seeking and recognizing God present and active in all things to the ends of the world and into the depths of history . . . *Evangelii gaudium*, the joy of proclaiming the Gospel, which is the mission of the Church and of the Society in the Church and in the world.

Dear Father Adolfo, you have experienced in your life that joy to which our brother, the Vicar of Christ, invites us. It can be seen in your peaceful wisdom. Thank you for guiding and accompanying us to this day and in this spirit as the Body of the Society of Jesus.

Thank you and Godspeed. May the Lord continue to accompany you always. Our prayers go with you as well.

Rome, 3 October 2016
Federico Lombardi, S.J.

HOMILY

Fr. Bruno Cadoré, O.P.
Church of the Gesù, Rome, 2 October 2016

Readings: Ha 1, 2–3; 2, 2–4; Ps 94; 2 Tm 1, 6–8.13–14; Lk 17, 5–10

Lord, increase our faith!

This pressing request to the Lord is the most beautiful prayer one can imagine to "open" the celebration of your General Congregation. And in the Gospel that has just been proclaimed, Jesus points out two reasons why this prayer is so right. This faith is necessary—even if it remains as modest in appearance as a mustard seed—because it is about daring to aim for the improbable: "you can say to this mulberry tree, be uprooted and planted in the sea, and it will obey you." It is even more necessary, because it is to understand that, even if we aim for the incredible, it is about daring to say: "We are unworthy servants: we have only done our duty"! An assembly such as yours, rooted in a tradition of such rich evangelization, carrier of so many and such varied experiences, will without doubt move between the duty of constantly calling the Society to dare the audacity of the "improbable" and the evangelical willingness to do it, with the humility of those who know that, in this service where the human engages all his energy, "everything depends on God."

But is it possible for us to have this audacity of the improbable?—This audacity of the Gospel, the audacity of your founder Ignatius who founded his Society, small as a mustard seed, in a time of crisis, of a need for brotherhood and faced with immense challenges? It is, it seems to me, the question which torments the prophet Habakkuk, "How long Lord, must I call for help, but you do not listen? or cry out to you, Violence!, but you do not save?" Many among you could list the curses of the Prophet which explain the strength with which he calls on his God. Still today the world is disfigured by those who accumulate what is not theirs, who pursue first their own interests, who build a world on the blood of a multitude of forgotten and manipulated people, who continuously invent new idols. Violence, which disfigures the face of the human in individuals, in societies, and in peoples. The most improbable thing, in this context, may not be to reverse, with our human hands and within the limits of our minds and our capacities, these acts of violence so as to reset the world. We must, of course, dare to seek how to mend what is torn. But the real audacity of the improbable: is it not to make heard, at the heart of this work of "re-sewing," the voice of the One who against all odds, led his people and gave them the strength to live by his faithfulness? May the Lord grant you the grace, throughout your reflections and discernment, to be guided, engendered, in this audacity to make known through your commitments, your words, your solidarity, the always unexpected voice of the One in whom the world hopes, who reverses death and establishes life, the One to whom you seek to give the greatest glory?

Far from being naive, this audacity is realistic. Paul the Apostle, in his Second Letter to Timothy, helps us to understand why. It is a realistic audacity, first, because it is based on a primary gift: "rekindle the gift of God," an invitation that echoes others formulated by the apostle: "Never flag in zeal, be aglow with the Spirit, serve the Lord" (Rm 12, 11); "Do not quench the Spirit" (1 Th 5, 19); "Do not grieve the Holy Spirit" (Eph 4, 29). This is probably the main task of a Congregation such as the one that opens for you today: to draw on the audacity of the improbable in fidelity to the work of the Spirit. To find the strength and creativity of fidelity in the breath in which the Spirit holds us as he leads us to encounter and to listen to the other, creates a well of compassion in the heart of the person, and consolidates the unbreakable alliance with those who are entrusted to us. But this audacity of the improbable is realistic also because it seeks constantly to be in union with the One of whom Paul, enduring his suffering, is made herald, apostle, and doctor, the Savior Jesus Christ who has done the improbable when he destroyed death and made life and immortality shine through the Gospel (v. 9–12). The audacity of evangelization is oriented towards the face of this Savior whose voice it seeks to make heard and whose mystery it seeks to make known. The mystery of this voice is that its only claim is to affirm that it is in the humble confrontation with the absurd, that the life given up opens in this world the path of a new birth to life.

Increase our faith, asked the apostles. But, how did this request come to them? How, in our time, are we to respond to the urgent need to live as men of faith, contemplatives in action, men whose lives will truly be given for others? You remember that in the Gospel of Luke, the passage that we have heard today comes after Jesus's teaching about life shared between brothers. It is inevitable that scandals happen, and you must be on your guard not to lead even one of these little ones into sin. Then comes the teaching on forgiveness tirelessly given to the brother, once, seven times . . . And then comes the request of the apostles! Deep down, it is always the same thing: just like the Kingdom, the unlikely is never far from you. Yes, of course, it is a passionate search to open up ways for wisdom in this world, paths on which human words and projects bear meaning in trying to build a hospitable world for human beings. But what can be offered as the inner fire for this passionate search, is the concrete experience, sometimes so banal and often so difficult, of forgiveness. This experience of going beyond the offense in order to give, again, without condition, life in abundance. This experience which makes us discover that in ourselves we have a life that is so much stronger, so much more beautiful, than the one we thought we possessed, a life that finds its full truth when it breaks away from the self to be offered to the other. This is the experience of community life, the witness to which is so important today. It seems to me that it is not for nothing that in the Gospel of today, Jesus continues by recalling this simple servant. Of what, precisely, are you the servant? Of a table, a table of sinners, a table of welcome for all, to which are invited the blind and the lame, Pharisees and publicans, adulterers and good people. Your founder, Ignatius, prayed like this: "Lord Jesus, teach us to be generous, teach us to serve You as You deserve, to give and not to count the cost, to fight and not to heed the wounds, to toil and not to seek for rest, to labor and to ask for no reward save that of knowing we are doing Your will." Is this not an invitation, once more today, to place ourselves, all of us, at the service of this table?

The table of Emmaus, where the simple servant learns his mission by allowing himself to be guided by his first companion, the Savior, Jesus Christ.

Lord, increase our faith!

HOMILY

Fr. James E. Grummer, S.J. Mass of the Holy Spirit
Church of Santo Spirito in Sassia, Rome, 14 October 2016

Readings: 1 Cor. 12: 3b–7, 12–13; Jn 20:19–23

St. Ignatius left almost nothing in writing about the Holy Spirit, except in his personal notebook during his deliberations on poverty. Now, maybe he was just being prudent, because, after all, some of his contemporaries thought he looked and sounded like one of the *alumbrados*. You remember them from history class in the novitiate: the enlightened heretics who claimed to have direct channels of communication with, and direct revelations from, the Holy Spirit. Based on the appearance of things, various inquisitors investigated St. Ignatius in at least eight formal processes before 1545, when he informed the king of Portugal that he had spent 64 days in different prisons as a suspected heretic.

Since St. Ignatius referred to the Holy Spirit so seldom in his writings, the few times we find a quotation are all the more precious. In the *Spiritual Exercises,* he refers directly to the Holy Spirit only six times, and five of these references are quotations from the scriptures that occur in the supplemental material for contemplating the Mysteries of Christ our Lord. One of those direct quotations presents points for praying over the Gospel passage we just heard. Let me quote #304 this morning, because in the three points that St. Ignatius presents, we have a good lens for considering the Holy Spirit whose aid we seek during this Eucharist. (1) The disciples were assembled "through fear of the Jews," (2) "Jesus appeared to them when the doors were locked. He stood in their midst and said, 'Peace be with you,'" and (3) "He gives them the Holy Spirit, saying to them, 'Receive the Holy Spirit; whose sins you forgive are forgiven them.'" We can see that the movement Ignatius proposes in these three points is quite simple: a journey from Fear to Joy and from Gift to Mission, a journey for every Jesuit and for every General Congregation.

One might say that there is some fear involved in what we do today and throughout the coming days. Maybe we are afraid of spending the rest of our lives in small group discussions or sitting in the Aula with headphones. More seriously, the *De statu* report outlines daunting challenges that might fill us with fear—the problems of the individual human heart, the Society of Jesus, the Church, and the world today can frighten us. Maybe we are afraid of asking one of those among us to bear the office of General on behalf of all the rest, or maybe we are just afraid of what the new General might have to say about a new assignment.

However, fears are as numerous as they are useless. More important is the joy that accompanies every experience of the Risen Lord who displaces whatever fears we might feel. Time and again, in life and ministry, we have experienced the Risen Lord in his wounded hands and side, in the least of our brothers and sisters, in the brokenness of our companions and friends in the Lord. We joyfully experienced the Lord Crucified and Risen in one another during the past week of reflection and prayer together, in meeting old friends and making new friends in the Lord. In spite of, or perhaps even because of our fears, Jesus fills us with joy.

Joy is only one of the gifts we receive from the Risen Lord. This past week we received the gift of recognizing the action of the Spirit in the Society and the Church and the world, in every human heart. We have deepened our appreciation of the gift of membership in a group committed to struggle beneath the banner of the Cross. The *Contemplatio ad amorem* asks us to reflect on the gifts we have received so that we can freely put them at the service of the Giver who so wants to heal and bless a fallen world. So many gifts, like the ceaseless flow of a waterfall or the fountains in St. Peter's Square!

As if the gifts of creation, redemption, and sanctification were not enough, the Gospel recounts the great gift of the Holy Spirit and the gift of reconciliation that has special meaning for members of priestly religious order like ours. Whether or not we are ordained, through baptism and religious profession we are agents of the God of Mercy, "ready to reconcile the estranged," as we read in the *Formula of the Institute*. During this Year of Mercy, today's Gospel has special relevance for reminding us to collaborate with the God who seeks out the lost sheep; who sweeps every corner of the house for the lost coin; who never ceases to put sandals on our feet, robes on our backs, and rings on our fingers.

Our mission this morning is to elect a general. We will be locked into an upper room, not for fear but for concentrated listening to the Spirit's whisper. We are not afraid because we believe so strongly that the Spirit guides the balloting that according to *Formula* 84 "The man elected cannot refuse the election." Our mission is to listen carefully, but also to trust that even if I need batteries in my spiritual hearing aid, I can trust that through this band of brothers the Spirit will identify the man he has chosen. We can trust that Jesus will give us his Spirit, no matter how locked up we may feel.

Actually, I doubt that cautious prudence kept Ignatius from referring to the Holy Spirit, for the Inquisition never intimidated him—he was joyful in what we might call Third Week moments. Writing to the Portuguese king about the Inquisition's procedures, he said, "not for all the temporal power and riches under heaven would I wish that all this had not befallen me; indeed, I wish far worse would befall me for the greater glory of his Divine Majesty." I believe Ignatius said so little about the Holy Spirit because he did not want words to distract doubters and Inquisitors from the deeds of the Spirit, from experiencing the joy, gifts, and mission that come to us from the Holy Spirit. Ignatius's silence about the Holy Spirit leaves more room for each individual to contemplate and experience the action of the Holy Spirit in a uniquely personal way.

As we celebrate the Eucharist at this altar this morning, may the Spirit fill our silence with joy and all the other gifts we need to embrace the special mission this day of choosing the one the Lord has chosen.

HOMILY

Fr. Arturo Sosa, S.J. Mass of Thanksgiving
Church of the Gesù, Rome
15 October 2016

Readings: Sir 39:6–10 (gr.); Rom. 15:2–7 ; 16, 17–18. 25–27; Mk 13:33–37

Dearest Brothers,

A few days ago, in this very Church of the Gesù, where lie the remains of St. Ignatius and Pedro Arrupe, Fr. Bruno Cadoré invited us to possess the audacity of the improbable as the distinctive mark of persons of faith, who seek to bear witness to such faith in the complex reality of human life. He invited us to leave fear behind and to row into the deep, as a way of being at the same time creative and faithful during the General Congregation.

Certainly, the audacity that we need in order to be servants of the mission of Christ Jesus can only flow from faith. For this reason, our gaze is directed first of all to God, since *we have but one Father in heaven*, as the passage from the Gospel which we have just heard reminds us. And as the *Formula of the Institute* reminds us in paragraph no.1: "[...] let (the Jesuit) take care, as long as he lives, first of all to keep before his eyes God and then the nature of this Institute." Indeed, it is with our whole heart that we wish to be in harmony with the Merciful Father, God who alone is Love, our Principle and Foundation. The heart of each of us and the heart of the body of the Society as well.

If our faith is like that of Mary, mother of Jesus and Mother of the Society of Jesus, our audacity can go even further and seek not just the improbable, but the impossible, because *nothing is impossible for God*, as the Archangel Gabriel proclaims in the scene of the Annunciation (Luke 1:37). It is the same faith of St. Theresa of Ávila or St. Theresa of Jesus, whose memorial we celebrate today. She too, without fear, entrusted herself to the Lord in order to undertake the improbable and the impossible.

Therefore, let us ask the Lord for this faith, so that we, as the Society of Jesus, can also make our own the words of Mary in her response to the extraordinary call she received: "Behold I am the handmaid of the Lord. May it be done to me according to your word." Like Ignatius and the First Companions, like so many Jesuit brothers who have fought and who fight *under the banner of the cross*, in service solely of the Lord and of his Church, we too desire to contribute to that which today seems impossible: a humanity reconciled in justice, that lives in peace, in a common home well-cared-for, where there is a place for all, because we recognize each other as brothers and sisters, sons and daughters of the same and only Father.

For this reason, we reaffirm even today the conviction of Ignatius as he wrote the Constitutions: "The Society was not instituted by human means; and it is not through them that it can be preserved and increased, but through the grace of the omnipotent hand of Christ our God and Lord. Therefore in him alone must be placed our hope."

With our hope placed in God and in God alone, the General Congregation will proceed with its deliberations and it will contribute to its duty *to preserve and grow this entire body* (*Const.* 719).

The preservation and growth of the body of the Society is tightly bound to the depth of the spiritual life of each of its members and of the communities in which we share life and mission with our companions. At the same time, it takes extraordinary intellectual depth to think creatively about the ways in which our service to the mission of Christ Jesus can be more effective, in the creative tension of the Ignatian *magis*. To think about how to understand in depth the moment of human history which we live, and to contribute to the search for alternatives for overcoming poverty, inequality, and oppression. To think so that we never cease to pose pertinent theological questions, and so deepen our understanding of the faith that we ask the Lord to increase in ourselves.

We are not alone. As companions of Jesus we too want to follow the way of the incarnation, to identify ourselves with the human beings who suffer the consequences of injustice. The Society of Jesus can grow only in collaboration with others, only if it becomes *the least Society that collaborates*. Let us be careful about linguistic pitfalls. We want to increase collaboration, not just to seek others to collaborate with us, with our works, because we do not want to lose the prestige of position of one who has the last word. We want to collaborate generously with others, inside and outside the Church, in the awareness, which comes from the experience of God, of being called to the mission of Christ Jesus, which does not belong to us exclusively, but which we share with so many men and women consecrated to the service of others.

In the journey of collaboration, with the grace of God, we will find new companions to increase our numbers as well, always much too small no matter how great: collaborators who, along with the others, are invited to be part of this body. There is no doubt about the need to increase our prayer and our work for vocations to the Society, and to continue the complex work of providing formation that would make of them true Jesuits, members of this multicultural body that is called to testify to the richness of interculturalism as the face of humanity, created in the image and likeness of God.

Today, let us therefore make our own the words of the apostle Paul: *May the God of endurance and encouragement grant you to think in harmony with one another, in keeping with Christ Jesus, that with one accord you may with one voice glorify the God and Father of our Lord Jesus Christ* (Rom. 15:5–6).

HOMILY

Fr. Arturo Sosa, S.J.
Closure of the General Congregation 36
Church of Sant'Ignazio, Rome
12 November 2016

Readings: 1 Jn 4, 7–16; Ps 144; Mk 16,15–20

At the end of a powerful experience of discernment we feel a sense of vertigo when faced with what should come after. We feel the difficulty of giving life to the choice made, of being converted to the way of proceeding that expresses the decision of following the breath of the Holy Spirit.

The *Spiritual Exercises* of Saint Ignatius sets the "Contemplation to Attain Love" as a transition into everyday life. A contemplation that resonates strongly in the first letter of the Apostle John, which we have just heard. God wishes to be known as the one who is Love. Therefore, He is made present to humanity in sending his Son, a gesture of love that gives us life, the only true life to which we aspire. God the Father puts into practice the two observations Saint Ignatius makes at the beginning of the contemplation: "Love ought to be shown more in deeds than in words," and "Love is an exchange where each one gives everything he has and is." The Lord has given himself completely, even to death on the cross, and remains with us daily until the end of the world, because he has given us his Spirit. Saint Ignatius invites us to ask for gratitude for so many gifts received, and so to move us in order that we too might give of ourselves entirely—*in all things to love and serve the Divine Majesty.*

This is the phrase that has guided our sessions in the Aula of the Congregation. Christ on the cross was present in our labors, to bring the discernment beyond our reasoning, our liking or disliking, in order to arrive at the consolation of being in harmony with the will of the Father. Jesus on the eve of his Passion went to the Mount of Olives and struggled in his prayer until his sweat became like drops of blood in order to accept the consequences of his mission, so far from what to him might have been gratifying or acceptable. Likewise, we were shaken by the testimony of our brothers in situations of war and so we were moved by love to cry out as one: "Take Lord, and receive all my liberty, my memory, my understanding, my will, all that I have and possess. You have given all to me. To you, O Lord, I return it. All is yours: dispose of it wholly according to your will. Give me your love and your grace, for this alone is enough for me."

In this General Congregation we also re-lived the experience of God's love, made present in ways so varied, in our personal lives and in our body as companions of Jesus. Yet again, the abundance, variety, and depth of his gifts have overwhelmed us. Everything we experienced was grace, free gift and surprising.

The discernment process of the Society gathered as General Congregation confronts us with the challenge of becoming ministers of reconciliation, in a world that did not stop turning during our deliberations. The wounds of war continue to deepen, the flow of refugees increases, the suffering of migrants crush us ever more, the Mediterranean has swallowed up dozens of people in the two months we have spent together. Inequalities between peoples and within nations are the sign of a world that scorns humanity. Politics, the "art" of negotiation so as to put the common good above particular interests, continues to deteriorate before our eyes. These particular interests, in fact, masked under the guise of nationalisms, elect leaders and make decisions that block the processes of integration and action as citizens of the world. Politics struggles to provide a humane way of making reasonable decisions, and renouncing appeals to the impositions of the powerful. The deep desire of the mothers and the children everywhere in the world to be able to have a life in peace, with social relations based on justice, seems to wither in the midst of conflicts and wars for reasons that corrode the love that makes life possible.

Our discernment leads us to see the world through the eyes of the poor and to work with them so that true life may grow. It invites us to go to the peripheries to seek to understand how to globally address the entirety of the crisis that denies minimum living conditions for the majority of humanity and threatens life on planet Earth, in order to open a space for the Good News. Our apostolate is, therefore, necessarily intellectual. The merciful eyes, which we received by identifying ourselves with Christ crucified, allow us to deepen our comprehension of all that oppresses men and women in our world. The signs that accompany our proclamation of the Gospel are those which correspond to casting out the demons of false understandings of reality. This is why we learn new languages, to grasp the lives of the different peoples and share the Good News of salvation for all. If we open our hearts to the Holy Spirit and our minds to the truth of God's love, we will not drink the poison of ideologies which justify oppression, violence among human beings, and the irrational exploitation of natural resources. Our faith in Christ, who died and rose, enables us to help out, along with many other men and women of good will, to help lay hands on this ailing world and to help in its healing.

Let us go then to preach the Gospel everywhere, consoled by the experience of the love of God who has gathered us into one as companions of Jesus. As with the first Fathers, the Lord has been propitious to us in Rome, and sends us to every part of the world and to all human cultures. We go in confidence because He works with us and confirms with new signs our life and mission.

GC 36: List of Participants

Family Name, First Name	Participation	From	Conference
Afiawari, Chukwuyenum A.	Elector	ANW	JES
Afulo, Joseph O.	Provincial	AOR	JES
Almeida, Miguel Nuno de	Elector	POR	EUR
Alonso Vicente, Pablo José	Elector	ESP	EUR
Alvarado López, Rolando E.	Provincial	CAM	PAL
Álvarez de los Mozos, Francisco Javier	Elector	ESP	EUR
Amalraj, Paramasivam Stanislaus	Provincial	AND	JCS
Assouad, Victor	Elector	PRO	EUR
Barrero Díaz, Joaquín	General Counselor	CUR	EUR
Béré, Paul	Elector	AOC	JES
Biron, Jean-Marc	Provincial	GLC	JCU
Bisson, J. Peter	Provincial	CDA	JCU
Bresciani, Ivan	Elector	SVN	EUR
Bürgler, Bernhard	Elector	ASR	EUR
Calderón Schmidt, Gustavo	Elector	ECU	PAL
Cancino Franklin, Alejandro Patricio	Elector	MEX	PAL
Cariou-Charton, Sylvain	Elector	GAL	EUR
Casalone, Carlo	Elector	ITA	EUR
Castro Fones, Pablo	Elector	CHL	PAL
Cecero, John J.	Provincial	UNE	JCU
Cela Carvajal, Jorge	Conference President	PAL	PAL
Chimhanda, Chiedza	Provincial	ZIM	JES
Chirveches Pinaya, Osvaldo A.	Provincial	BOL	PAL
Chiti, Peter Leonard	Elector	ZAM	JES
Chong, Che-chon John	Provincial	KOR	CAP
Chow Sau-yan, Stephen	Elector	CHN	CAP
Ciancimino, David S.	Elector	UNE	JCU
Collins, David J.	Elector	MAR	JCU
Consolmagno, Guy J.	Elector	JCU	JCU
Corcoran, Anthony J.	Elector	RUS	EUR
Correa Jaramillo, Carlos Eduardo	Provincial	COL	PAL
Correia, José Manuel Frazão	Provincial	POR	EUR
Costa, António Virgílio Oliveira e	Elector	ZIM	JES
Costantino, Joseph S.	Elector	UNE	JCU
Côté, Gabriel	Elector	GLC	JCU
Cribb, Ian	Elector	CAP	CAP
Cruzado Silveri, Miguel Gabriel	General Counselor	CUR	PAL
Curtin, Stephen	Elector	ASL	CAP
Cutinha, Jerome	Elector	JAM	JCS
Dardis, John	Conference President	EUR	EUR
Dartmann, Stefan	Elector	GER	EUR
D'Cruz, Wendell	Elector	BOM	JCS
D'Cunha, Vernon	Provincial	BOM	JCS

Family Name, First Name	Participation	From	Conference
de Roux Rengifo, Francisco José	Elector	COL	PAL
Del Campo Simonetti, Cristián	Provincial	CHL	PAL
Devadoss Mudiappasamy,	Elector	MDU	JCS
Díaz Marcos, Cipriano	Elector	ESP	EUR
D'Mello, Joseph A.	Elector	KAR	JCS
Dobbelstein, Thierry	Elector	BML	EUR
D'Souza, Lisbert	General Counselor	CUR	JCS
D'Souza, Stanislaus Jerome	Provincial	KAR	JCS
Dubovský, Peter	Elector	SVK	EUR
Dumortier, François-Xavier	Elector	GAL	EUR
Echarte Oñate, Ignacio	Major Official	CUR	EUR
Edema, James	Elector	JES	JES
Eidt, João Renato	Provincial	BRA	PAL
Etxeberria Sagastume, Juan José	Elector	ESP	EUR
Fernandes, George	Provincial	JAM	JCS
Fernandes, Stanislaus	Elector	PUN	JCS
Fernández Dávalos, David de Jesús	Elector	MEX	PAL
Francis Xavier Periyanayagam,	Elector	MDU	JCS
Freire Yánez, Gilberto	Provincial	ECU	PAL
Friedrich, Ryszard	Elector	PMA	EUR
Ganza Gasanana, Jean-Baptiste	Elector	RWB	JES
Garanzini, Michael J.	Member (*FGC* 7)	CUR	JCU
García Jiménez, José Ignacio	Elector	ESP	EUR
Gartland, James G.	Elector	CDT	JCU
Geisinger, Robert J.	Elector	CDT	JCU
Gonsalves, Francis	Elector	GUJ	JCS
Greene, Thomas P.	Elector	UCS	JCU
Grenet, Jean-Yves	Provincial	GAL	EUR
Grieu, Etienne	Elector	GAL	EUR
Grummer, James E.	General Counselor	CUR	JCU
Guiney, John K.	Elector	HIB	EUR
Hernandez, Jean-Paul	Elector	ITA	EUR
Herry Priyono, Bernardinus	Elector	IDO	CAP
Heru Prakosa, Yoannes Berchmans	Elector	IDO	CAP
Howard, Damian	Elector	BRI	EUR
Huang, Daniel Patrick L.	General Counselor	CUR	CAP
Hurtado Durán, Manuel Gilberto	Elector	BOL	PAL
Hussey, Robert M.	Provincial	MAR	JCU
Iznardo Almiñana, Francisco	Elector	CAM	PAL
Janin, Franck	Provincial	BML	EUR
Jebamalai Irudayaraj L.,	Elector	MDU	JCS
Jeerakassery, Sebastian J.	Elector	DEL	JCS
Jeyaraj, Veluswamy	Provincial	CCU	JCS
Kajiyama, Yoshio	Provincial	JPN	CAP

Family Name, First Name	Participation	From	Conference
Keller, Herbert B.	Elector	MAR	JCU
Kesicki, Timothy P.	Conference President	JCU	JCU
Kiechle, Stefan	Provincial	GER	EUR
Kolacz, Jakub	Provincial	PME	EUR
Kot, Tomasz	General Counselor	CUR	EUR
Kowalczyk, Dariusz	Elector	PMA	EUR
Kujur, Joseph Marianus	Provincial	RAN	JCS
Kurien, Francis	Provincial	HAZ	JCS
Kyungu Musenge, Rigobert	Elector	ACE	JES
Lado Tonlieu, Ludovic	Elector	AOC	JES
Lamanna, Thomas J.	Elector	ORE	JCU
Lawler, Thomas A.	Provincial	WIS	JCU
Layden, Thomas	Provincial	HIB	EUR
Lee Hua, John	Provincial	CHN	CAP
Lenk, Martin	Elector	ANT	PAL
Lewis, Michael	Conference President	JES	JES
Lobo, John Wilfred	Elector	DAR	JCS
Lombardi, Federico	General Counselor	CUR	EUR
Loua, Zaoro Hyacinthe	Provincial	AOC	JES
Lozuk, Anto	Elector	CRO	EUR
Luna Pastore, Alberto Cristóbal	Elector	PAR	PAL
Magadia, José Cecilio	General Counselor	CUR	CAP
Magaña Aviña, José Francisco	Provincial	MEX	PAL
Magro, Patrick	Elector	MAL	EUR
Malvaux, Benoît	Major Official	CUR	EUR
Mangai, Varghese Poulose	Elector	CCU	JCS
Manickam, Irudayaraj	Elector	GUJ	JCS
Manwelo, Paulin	Elector	ACE	JES
Marcouiller, Douglas W.	General Counselor	CUR	JCU
Maruthukunnel, Jose Jacob	Elector	KER	JCS
Masawe, Fratern	General Counselor	CUR	JES
Mascarenhas, Agnelo	Elector	GOA	JCS
Matarazzo, Gianfranco	Provincial	ITA	EUR
McCarthy, John W.	Elector	CDA	JCU
McClain, J. Thomas	Major Official	CUR	JCU
McCoy, Brian	Provincial	ASL	CAP
McFarland, Michael C.	Elector	UNE	JCU
Mercier, Ronald A.	Provincial	UCS	JCU
Mesa Baquero, José Alberto	Member (*FGC* 7)	CUR	PAL
Migacz, Andrzej	Elector	PME	EUR
Minaku Lukoli, José	Provincial	ACE	JES
Minj, Francis	Elector	RAN	JCS
Minj, Kalyanus	Provincial	MAP	JCS
Minj, Santosh	Elector	HAZ	JCS

Family Name, First Name	Participation	From	Conference
Morante Buchhammer, Juan Carlos	Provincial	PER	PAL
Moreno, Antonio F.	Provincial	PHI	CAP
Morgalla, Stanislaw	Elector	PME	EUR
Mumba, Emmanuel	Provincial	ZAM	JES
Mutholil, George	Provincial	KER	JCS
Nebres, Bienvenido F.	Elector	PHI	CAP
Ngo, Chi Van	Elector	CFN	JCU
Nguyên Hai Tính, Francis Xavier	Elector	VIE	CAP
Nicolás, Adolfo	Fr General	CUR	CAP
Odiaka, Jude O.	Provincial	ANW	JES
Oh, In-don Francisco	Elector	KOR	CAP
O'Keefe, Joseph M.	Elector	UNE	JCU
Oliveira, Pedro Rubens Ferreira de	Elector	BRA	PAL
Orobator, Agbonkhianmeghe Emmanuel	Elector	AOR	JES
Ortmann, Tomasz	Provincial	PMA	EUR
Palacio Larrauri, Alfonso Carlos	Elector	BRA	PAL
Pallippalakatt, Varghese	Provincial	DUM	JCS
Pandikattu, Kuruvilla	Elector	DUM	JCS
Parmar, Francis	Provincial	GUJ	JCS
Pathirana, Angelo Sujeeva	Elector	SRI	JCS
Pattery, George	Conference President	JCS	JCS
Paul, Claudio	Elector	BRA	PAL
Paulson, Brian G.	Provincial	CDT	JCU
Peraza Celis, Arturo Ernesto	Provincial	VEN	PAL
Perekkatt, Varkey	Provincial	DEL	JCS
Pham, Hung T.	Elector	UCS	JCU
Pham Thanh Liêm, Joseph	Provincial	VIE	CAP
Power, Stephen	Elector	EUR	EUR
Preston, Dermot	Provincial	BRI	EUR
Pudota, Rayappa John Susai Raj	Elector	AND	JCS
Puig Puig, Llorenç	Elector	ESP	EUR
Rabeson, Solofonirina Jocelyn	Elector	MDG	JES
Raj, Susai	Elector	PAT	JCS
Ramos, Eudson	Elector	PAL	PAL
Ranaivoarson, (Pierre André)	Provincial	MDG	JES
Raper, Mark	Conference President	CAP	CAP
Rasiah, Jeyaraj	Provincial	SRI	JCS
Ratsimbazafy, Fulgence	Elector	MDG	JES
Ravizza, Mark A.	Elector	CFN	JCU
Ribeiro, Elton Vitoriano	Elector	BRA	PAL
Roca Alcázar, Fernando	Elector	PER	PAL
Rocha, Rosario	Provincial	GOA	JCS
Rodríguez Tamayo, Gabriel Ignacio	General Counselor	CUR	PAL

Family Name, First Name	Participation	From	Conference
Ruiz Pérez, Francisco José	Provincial	ESP	EUR
Rutishauser, Christian Michael	Elector	HEL	EUR
Sakuma, Tsutomu	Elector	JPN	CAP
Sansare, Bhausaheb	Provincial	PUN	JCS
Santarosa, Scott R.	Provincial	ORE	JCU
Sarmento, Joaquim Francisco da Silva	Elector	ETR	CAP
Sarralde Delgado, Luis Javier	Elector	COL	PAL
Sebasti L., Raj	Provincial	MDU	JCS
Siebner, Johannes	Elector	GER	EUR
Smolich, Thomas H.	Member (*FGC* 7)	CUR	JCU
Sosa Abascal, Arturo Marcelino	General Counselor	CUR	PAL
Spadaro, Antonio	Elector	ITA	EUR
Standaert, Nicolas	Elector	BSE	EUR
Stegman, Thomas D.	Elector	WIS	JCU
Stuchly, Josef	Elector	BOH	EUR
Sugiyo Pitoyo, Agustinus	Elector	IDO	CAP
Sunu Hardiyanta, Petrus	Provincial	IDO	CAP
Susaimanickam, Arul	Elector	KHM	JCS
Talos, Marius	Elector	ROM	EUR
Tigga, Boniface	Elector	PAT	JCS
Tigga, Ranjit	Elector	MAP	JCS
Tilve, Alejandro	Provincial	ARU	PAL
Torres Santos, Luis Orlando	Elector	UCS	JCU
Tshering, Kinley Joseph	Provincial	DAR	JCS
Tustonjic, Ante	Provincial	CRO	EUR
Uher, Rudolf	Provincial	SVK	EUR
Vadassery, Jose J.	Provincial	PAT	JCS
van Drunen, Theo	Elector	NER	EUR
Vaz, Dionysius	Elector	KAR	JCS
Vaz, Thomas	Elector	JCS	JCS
Velasco, Luis Rafael	Elector	ARU	PAL
Veramendi Espinoza, Johnny José	Elector	VEN	PAL
Verschueren, Johan	Provincial	BSE	EUR
Vidal González, Javier	Provincial	ANT	PAL
Vitkus, Gintaras	Elector	LIT	EUR
Vizi, Elemér	Elector	HUN	EUR
Weiler, Michael F.	Provincial	CFN	JCU
Xess, Ajit Kumar	Elector	RAN	JCS
Younès, Dany	Provincial	PRO	EUR

Index

Acta 15, 17n5, 19n14, 22n24, 25n34, 28n4, 30n8, 32n17
ad providentiam (assistant) 3, 6, 9, 11, 13, 15
admonitor for general 13
Alonso Vicente, Pablo José 15
Althann, Robert 3
alumbrados 73
Álvarez de los Mozos, Francisco Javier 11
Amalraj, Paramasivam Stanislaus 11
Amoris laetitia 22n27, 56, 61
apostolic life 24–27, 60, 66
apostolic works 1, 35
aprovechamiento 46, 47
Aquinas, Thomas, Saint 56
Arriaga, Rodrigo de 56n20
Arrupe, Pedro 49, 76
assessment instruments 35
assistancies 11, 13
Assouad, Victor 13
audacity 8, 12, 21, 26, 53, 54, 59, 70, 71, 76
Autobiography 18n9, 49

Barrero, Joaquín 3, 13
Benedict XVI (pope) 45
Béré, Paul 4, 5, 9
Biron, Jean-Marc 11
Blattert, Clemens 4, 8
Bonaventure, Saint 56
Borgia, Francis, Saint 3, 46, 50
business phase 12, 14

Cadoré, Bruno 8, 12, 26n39,
   homily of 70–72
Calls 4, 10
casuistry 56
Catechism of the Catholic Church 56

Cela, Jorge 4, 5, 9, 11
Civiltà cattolica, La 19n11, 50n13
clericalism 60, 62
Code of Canon Law 15, 42n10, 42n11
Code of Canons of the Eastern Churches (1990) 42n10, 42n11
Coetus praevius 3, 4, 5, 6
collaboration 10, 14, 23, 25, 27–35, 77
colonization 54, 58
Commission on Renewed Governance in the Service of Renewed Mission 5, 6, 10, 14
Commission on the Renewal of Jesuit Life and Mission 5, 6, 7, 10, 12, 14
common fund 31
communications strategy 31, 35
Companions in a Mission of Reconciliation and Justice (Decree 1) 14, 17, 19, 21, 23, 25
Complementary Norm (351) 33n21 52
Complementary Norm (362) 3, 11, 15, 42,
Complementary Norm (396) 15, 43
Comprehensive Review of Central Governance 29, 35
Conference of Latin America 12–13
conference presidents 4, 31
Conferences of Major Superiors 15, 32
Congregation for Divine Worship 55
Congregation of Procurators 15, 35, 67
congregation to elect vicar general 15
consolation 8, 14, 18, 20, 25, 27, 38, 40, 41, 48, 49, 52, 60, 61, 64, 78
Consolmagno, Guy J. 4
Constitutions 12, 15, 18n10, 19n12, 21n18, 21n19, 42, 43, 46, 77
   modifications of 701 and 704 42–43
Contemplatio ad amorem 17, 74
Coordinating Committee 5, 6, 7, 11

Côté, Gabriel 8

creation 14, 17, 21–22, 24, 26, 48, 74

Cribb, Ian 4

Cross of Christ 22, 40–41, 48–49, 50–52, 59, 64, 74, 76, 78

Cruzado, Miguel 4, 6, 10

Curia Generalizia 3

Curtin, Stephen 7

D'Cunha, Vernon 13

D'Souza, Lisbert 3,6, 9, 12, 13

Dalits 23

Dall'Oglio, Paolo 39

Danieluk, Robert 3

Dardis, John 4, 7, 9, 13, 15

Dartmann, Stefan 4, 6

de Certeau, Michel 49

de Lubac, Henri 48

de' Nobili, Roberto 55

Delegate for the Roman Houses 12, 13

Deputation on the State of the Society (*De statu Societatis*) 5–6, 7, 10, 13

discernment 1, 2, 5, 8, 9, 13, 14, 16, 18, 19, 20, 22, 26, 27, 28, 30, 32, 33, 34, 35, 38, 47, 48, 49, 50, 51, 52, 53, 55, 56, 57, 59, 62, 63, 70, 78, 79

apostolic 14, 19, 27, 32, 33, 35

communal 1, 8, 19, 20

Domus Interprovinciales Romanae (Interprovincial houses in Rome) 15, 41

Dufka, Vlastimil 8

Dumortier, Francois-Xavier 11

Echarte, Ignacio 4, 7, 13

ecology 14, 23

Edema, James 4

election

of assistant secretaries 11

of assistants *ad providentiam* 13

of coordinating committee 6

of secretary of congregation 9, 10, 11

of superior general 8, 9, 10, 11, 42, 74

election phase 12, 65

electors 4, 7, 8, 9, 10, 11, 12

environmental crises 17, 24

Evangelii gaudium (Pope Francis) 17n6, 20n15, 22n26, 26n36, 26n37, 61, 62, 69

Examen 12, 21

examiners 9

Fassett, Edward 7

Favre, Pierre 47, 51

Mémorial 49n10, 51n14

fears 73

Fernández, David 4

financial effectiveness and equity 35

first companions 14, 18, 20, 39, 46, 47, 49, 76

first plenary session 3, 7, 8

Formula of the Institute 21n18, 24n33, 39, 46, 76

Formulae 29, 35, 42

Francis (pope) 1, 3, 9, 14, 17, 19, 20, 21, 22, 24, 25, 26, 27n2, 34, 45, 53

address to General Congregation 45

casuistry 56

clericalism 60, 62

consolation 60, 61, 64

dialogue with Jesuits 53–64

digitalization 63

discernment 53–57, 59, 62, 63

environmental and social crises 17

Evangelii gaudium 17n6, 20n15, 22n26, 26n36, 26n37, 61, 62, 69

globalization and inculturation 54, 64

Jesuit wisdom 58

Laudato si' 17n2, 24n29, 48, 59, 60, 61

liquidity and unemployment 63

local vocations 62, 63

martyrdom and Jesuits 59

missionary expansion and colonization 54, 55

morality 54–56

politics 57–59

poverty 60

prophetic audacity 53, 54

Scholasticism 56

wars and exploitation 58

young people 59, 62, 63

fundamentalism 14, 23

Garanzini, Michael 12
García Jiménez, José Ignacio 7, 10
Gasanana, Jean-Baptiste Ganza 15
Geisinger, Robert 6
General Council 4, 13, 42, 43
General Councilor for Discernment and
    Apostolic Planning 13
General Councilor for Formation 13
General Curia 16, 29, 45, 66
General Examen 47
globalization 54
Gonsalves, Francis 6, 7, 10
governance 5–7, 10, 13–14, 27,
Greene, Thomas 4, 6
Grummer, James 3, 4, 6, 8, 11, 12
    homily of 73–75
*Guidelines for the Relationship between the
    Superior and the Director of Work*
    32, 36
Guiney, John 11

Häring, Bernard 56n22
healing 24, 40, 51, 79
Homily (Pope Francis) 45n4, 52n16
Homily of Father General Arturo Sosa
    25n35
Huang, Daniel 3, 4, 13
humanity 14, 23–24, 64, 68, 77–79
Hurtado, Albert, Saint 48

Ignatian spirituality 21, 22, 47
inculturation 54, 64
indigenous peoples 14, 23, 54, 55
integration 5, 6, 23, 25, 33, 79

Jesuit Refugee Service 12, 37
Jesuits
    community 10, 14, 19, 33
    key features of governance 14
    killed in service 39, 41
    vocation 10, 22, 39, 40, 45, 48, 59
    in zones of war and violence 15, 37
John Paul II (pope) 45, 53
joy 2, 17, 18, 19, 22, 48, 49, 50, 59, 65,
    67, 69, 73, 74
Jubilee of Mercy 11, 50, 74

Juridical Commission 6, 7
justice 1, 14, 17–18, 22–24, 34, 39, 47,
    49, 64, 76, 79

Kerhuel, Antoine 3, 13
Kesicki, Timothy 4, 6, 9
Kolvenbach, Peter-Hans 19n14, 30n48
Kot, Tomasz 4, 12, 13
Kumar, Prem 39
Kurien, Francis 6

Lado, Ludovic 7
language preferences 8
Larrauri, Alfonso Carlos Palacio 6, 12
Laudato si' (Pope Francis) 17n2, 24n29,
    48, 59, 60, 61
Leitner, Severin 4
"Letter Convoking General Congregation
    36" (Nicolás) 22n24
Lewis, Michael 4, 6, 11
Life of Saint Ignatius of Loyola
    (Ribadeneyra) 50n13
Liturgy Committee 4
local superiors 15, 19, 31, 33, 34, 36
Logistics Committee 3
Lombardi, Federico 7, 9, 11, 69
Loyola, Ignatius of, Saint 21, 26, 27,
    38n2, 46–51, 60, 61, 68, 70, 72–74,
    76–78
Lozuk, Anto 11

Magadia, José 4, 13
    magis 26, 47, 53, 54, 67, 77
    major superiors 4, 15, 19, 31, 32, 33,
        41, 42, 43, 66
Malvaux, Benoît 6, 11
Manwelo, Paulin 10
Marcouiller, Douglas 4, 6, 13
marginalization 24
marginalized peoples 23. *See also*
    indigenous peoples
Masawe, Fratern 4, 13
Mascarenhas, Agnelo 9, 11
McCarthy, John 7
McClain, Thomas, 4
Mémorial (Favre) 49n10, 51n14

Mesa, José Alberto 12

"Message for the Celebration of the Day of Peace" (Paul VI) 39n5

migrants 5, 23, 25, 79

migration 14

ministry
  among indigenous peoples 14
  collaboration and 28
  integral element in Jesuits 28
  of friendship 39
  of justice and peace 23
  of reconciliation 17–19, 22
  networking and 31

minors 15, 41, 66, 67

Misericordiae vultus 17n6

Missio Dei 27, 34

Monumenta Nadal 46n5, 48n9

Moreno, Antonio 4, 6, 15

Mudiappasamy, Devadoss 11

Mulemi, Patrick 3, 9

Musenge, Rigobert Kyungu 3, 6

Nadal, Jerónimo 46, 48

Nebres, Bienvenido F. 6, 11, 12

networking 14, 27, 29, 30, 31, 34

networks 25, 29, 31, 33, 39

Nicolás, Adolfo 3, 17, 21, 22n24, 25, 28n3, 30, 65, 69
  three types of Jesuits for 67
  words of gratitude to 65–69

Order of Preachers, 15

Orobator, Agbonkhianmeghe, 12, 13, 18, 19

Ouellet, Mark Cardinal, 27

Paranhos, Washington 8

Parmar, Francis 6

parresía 53, 54

Pattery, George 4, 6

Paul VI (pope) 45, 48
  "Message for the Celebration of the Day of Peace" 39n5

Paul, Claudio 13

Periyanayagam, Francis Xavier 4, 10

Philippines Province 13

politics 57–59

Postulate Committee 3, 6

poverty 18, 24, 25, 31, 38, 46, 51, 60, 73, 77

Power, Stephen 4

Practica quaedam 35

Priyono, Bernardinus Herry 7

Promotio iustitiae 24n30–n31, 39n4

prophetic audacity 53, 54

province congregations 1, 3, 4, 5, 14

province structures 35

Qoheleth 20

Raj, Sebasti L. 7

Ramos, Eudson 4

Raper, Mark 4

Ravizza, Mark 7, 15

recommendations 15, 27, 29–30, 35–36

reconciliation 1, 5, 14, 17–19, 21–25, 37, 39, 41, 64, 74, 79

refugees 23, 25, 79. *See also* migrants

regional assistants 12, 13, 31

"Réhabiliter la politique" 57

Relatio praevia 10

Renewed Governance for Renewed Mission 10, 14

restructuring, of provinces and regions 31

Ribadeneyra, Pedro de
  The Life of Saint Ignatius of Loyola 50n13

Ricci, Matteo 55

Rodríguez, Gabriel Ignacio 3, 7, 9, 13

Rodríguez, Jesús 3

Rotelli, Gian Giacomo 3

Rupnik, Marko 9

Sacrament of Reconciliation 21

Salis, Fabrizio 7

Santarosa, Scott 11

Sarralde Delgado, Luis Javier 6

Scholasticism 56

Secretariat Committee 4

Secretary of the Congregation 9, 10, 11

Sectoral Secretaries 31

secularization 22

situationalism 56
Smolich, Thomas W. 12
social crises, 17, 24
Sosa, Arturo 2, 3, 7, 12, 13, 25
  Francis (pope) 63
  homily in closure of Thirty-Sixth
    General Congregation by 78–79
  homily of, Mass of Thanksgiving 76–77
Spadaro, Antonio 12
Spain 13, 63
Spiritual Exercises 1, 8, 17n3, 21, 24n32,
    38n1, 48, 49, 50, 73, 78
spiritus vertiginis 48
Standaert, Nicolas 6, 11
Stegman, Thomas 10
superior general 2, 5, 12, 42, 43, 63, 65
  election of 8, 9, 10, 11, 42, 74
  resignation of 43
superiors and directors of works 34

Thirty-Fifth General Congregation 45n3,
    65, 66
Thirty-Second General Congregation 45
Thirty-Sixth General Congregation 1, 3,
    16, 21, 45, 53, 63
Torres, Luis Orlando 11, 12, 16
training for leadership 35

Union of Superiors General 67

Van der Lugt, Frans, 39
Vatican II 29, 54, 56n22, 61
Vaz, Thomas 4
Velasco, Luís Rafael 7
Venice 14, 18, 19, 26
vicar 8, 9, 10, 11, 12, 15
violence 17, 23, 37, 39, 40, 41, 70, 79

war and violence 37, 39, 41
witness 2, 14–15, 19, 37–39, 76

Xavier, Francis 40

Yogyakarta 3
Yong, Kenneth 7
Younès, Dany 15
Yuraszeck, José 8